NAVIGATING
THE TIBER

Fr. Brian,
God bless
your priesthood!

NAVIGATING
THE TIBER

How to Help Your
Friends and Family
Journey Toward the
Catholic Faith

DEVIN ROSE

Catholic
Answers
Press

Navigating the Tiber
© 2016 by Devin Rose

Unless otherwise noted, biblical citations are taken from the Revised Standard Version of the Bible (© 1971 by Division of Christian Education of the National Council of the Churches of Christ in the United States of America).

Published by Catholic Answers, Inc.
2020 Gillespie Way
El Cajon, California 92020
1-888-291-8000 orders
619-387-0042 fax
catholic.com

Printed in the United States of America

Cover design by Devin Schadt
Interior design by Claudine Mansour Design

ISBNs
978-1-941663-77-6
978-1-941663-78-3 Kindle
978-1-941663-79-0 ePub

To George Martinez

CONTENTS

INTRODUCTION

A Vexing River

Since its founding along the Tiber in the eighth century B.C., Rome has been identified with that unruly river. Thousands of years later, the phrase "Crossing the Tiber" came to be used for the conversion of Protestants to Catholicism. I made my crossing in 2001, and since then have had the honor of accompanying many friends and family along theirs.

Historically, the Tiber's flooding and silt meant trouble for Roman mariners. The spiritual journey across the river to the Catholic Church is often no less tricky for our Protestant friends. How can we help them chart the right course? How can we journey with them, to help them understand the Church and consider its claims? In this book I hope to answer those questions.

EQUIPPING YOUR SHIP

Before we begin, understand that it is not enough just to learn apologetics arguments and lay them on your friends. Much more is required, beginning at the human level with friendship. If you are not first and foremost a good friend (or brother, sister, son, etc.), then no amount of brilliant apologetics will help you. The perception of the message's quality is influenced by the character of the messenger. The important thing to remember is that, whether or not your friend becomes Catholic, you value his friendship and earnestly desire his good. Keep that in mind when the discussion starts getting heated and tense. St. Peter, the first pope, directed Christians to do exactly this in 1 Peter 3:15: "Always be prepared to make a defense to any one who calls you to account for the

READ TO SUCCEED

Throughout this book you will find references to other works, whether online articles or books. Each one of these goes into greater detail on a particular topic we discuss.

No one book can equip you in-depth on 2,000 years of history and theology. But when you come across a topic in this book, or in your discussions with Protestant friends, that you want to delve into more deeply, check out one of my recommendations.

Also, your Protestant friends may suggest books for you to read. Feel free to do so, but be prepared to read with a critical eye. Many Protestant books that argue against Catholicism do so with misconceptions, errors, and inaccuracies. It can take even a trained apologist substantial time to dismantle the flaws and problems in such books, and to one less seasoned it can be impossible to distinguish the wheat from the chaff. If you do get stumped, I have suggestions for you later on in how to deal with it.

hope that is in you, yet *do it with gentleness and reverence.*"

Do you read the Bible? If not, start to now! Both Old and New Testaments are important, but the New Testament is primary. If you are a good self-starter, just dive in and start reading the New Testament. If you need more guidance, look for a good Bible study at a nearby parish or go to a Catholic bookstore and ask if it carries individual Bible study guides.

Reading the Bible serves two purposes. First, you will benefit from reading the inspired word of God, coming to know Christ more deeply. Second, you will grow in familiarity with the books of the Bible, their contents and authors, all of which will help you in your dialogue with your Protestant friends. Nothing makes you more credible in the eyes of Protestants than regular Bible reading. An Evangelical friend of mine once interrogated me and another Catholic friend at lunch and asked if we read the Bible often. I was able to say yes, and that carried significant weight in his mind. To fervent Protestants, a person who claims to be a Christian but who doesn't read the Bible is at best ignorant and at worst a hypocrite.

Another indispensable tool for your utility belt is the *Catechism of the Catholic Church* (CCC). This handy work distills 2,000 years of Catholic teaching into an accessible book, explaining the most important doctrines of the Church with supporting biblical verses and quotations from the Church Fathers, popes, and saints. Read through it all or use it as a topical resource for Catholic doctrine as well as a jumping-off point to go deeper in a particular area that interests you.

You should also go deeper into apologetics specifically by reading some of the books I suggest throughout this book and by listening to programs like Catholic Answers Live. By doing so you will broaden and deepen your understanding of the Faith and become well-versed in the most common argument and counter-arguments that arise in discussions with Protestants.

THE LAY OF THE LAND

As a Catholic hoping to lead your friend to full communion, you have the challenging task of not only learning your own Faith, but also coming to grips with the wide-ranging beliefs of Protestantism. Begin by learning what your friend believes by asking him questions. Get to know his theological ideas and the teachings of his denomination, and his own story of conversion to Christ. Knowing who you are talking to is a vital part of having a fruitful discussion. Nothing frustrates progress like misconceptions and unfounded prejudices— which can occur just as easily on both sides—so be on the lookout and dispel them as soon as you can.

Every journey by sea requires you to chart a course, and so this book is organized in a way that flows naturally from one argument or topic of conversation to the next, in an order that I have found to be the most effective. Of course, every conversation is different, and you should not be afraid when your discussion inevitably diverges from the course presented here. Just remember that if you start getting lost at sea, you can gently steer the conversation back to the key arguments presented here. Likewise, we will focus on the strongest and most common replies and counter-arguments that are encountered in dialogue, but it is impossible to foresee every response that your friend might make. Truly, I've heard some puzzling replies in my own discussions with friends! And I've also heard some that made me step back and really think. Friendship runs both ways. You must be willing to critically examine your own beliefs and be open to growth and deeper conversion. Expecting that of your friend but not of yourself is disingenuous.

Not all friends make good dialogue partners. Some are apathetic about the differences between themselves and Catholics. Others are so certain that their particular beliefs are correct that they see no point in discussing them with Catholics. You must gauge their level of interest, openness, and your degree of friendship to get a feel for where they are at and whether discussions with them would have a good chance of bearing fruit.

RED FLAGS

Many Protestants simply aren't interested in debating doctrines that they believe in, let alone examining the foundation that underlies those doctrines. They might be uninterested for a host of reasons: they are weak in their faith; they would never consider converting because it would hurt their family; they are sure they are in the truth; they subscribe to lowest common denominator Christianity and think Catholics and Protestants are both fine, so why worry; the list goes on.

You will be able to spot a person with such an attitude fairly easily. Once you try out several of the lures described below and get no bites from them—or worse, rebuffs—consider spending your time talking with another friend instead. You can't sail your ship in a dead calm, or fabricate a gust of wind to fill another ship's sails.

You will also run into Protestants who are virulently anti-Catholic. They may send you links or videos describing the pope as the Antichrist and the Catholic Church as the whore of Babylon from the book of Revelation. These kinds of Protestants have swallowed hook, line, and sinker a form of Protestant fundamentalism that makes them particularly hardened against Catholicism. That fact does not mean that you should avoid engaging them necessarily, but know that you are in for a difficult battle, one in which they will be extremely closed to listening to anything favorable toward the Church.

I talked with one friend of mine, Jeremiah, for several years about Catholicism. By the end of it, he understood the Catholic arguments well and how they were more plausible and consistent than those of Protestantism. Yet, he would not become Catholic. He came from an ethnic culture with strong family ties—not a bad thing at all!—and while his father and mother were still alive, he could never think about causing them pain by leaving their Protestant denomination. That's okay. I realized that for now we needed to put our discussions on the back-burner and just remain friends with each other. The time will come, God willing, when we can discuss these matters again, but I know that while his parents live, further discussions are not warranted.

CHOOSING YOUR LURE

Let's say, though, that your friend seems amenable to discussing these topics with you. How do you begin to engage them in dialogue?

LURE #1: *Be Open to Opportunities*

If your Protestant friend has not yet brought up anything about his beliefs or yours, it can be best to wait for a good opportunity to present itself to broach the subject. Look for current events in the world to talk about that pertain to faith or religion: the splitting of a Protestant denomination, the latest controversial thing that the pope said, a recent movie placing the Catholic Church in a negative light, the rise of Islamic terrorism, and so on. You can bring up the topic and ask what he thinks about it. In doing so, you learn more about him and his ideas, as well as which subjects interest him and which don't.

LURE #2: *Share Catholic Experiences from Your Own Life*

In friendships, you inevitably are sharing events from your own life. These events are ripe opportunities for discussing your faith with your friend. For instance, you can tell him you went to Mass, or eucharistic adoration (which most Protestants know nothing about), or that it is a traditional feast day of some saint or Catholic celebration (Epiphany, Pentecost, etc.). Not always, but sometimes, your friend will inquire into what you did, and that gives you an opportunity to share with him in a simple, factual way what it was about.

Note that you don't want to use the first time this happens as an opportunity to ambush them with five minutes of monologue about details of Catholicism. You want to whet their appetite, not utterly quench it. Gently explain with them what it is and a little of the background about it, and then see where the conversation goes. Over time, you will be able to share more, or go into more details, and deepen your mutual understanding of each other.

LURE #3: *Plant Seeds*

One friend of mine was fairly perplexed about Catholicism. He was an Evangelical Protestant of the Southern Baptist variety, and to him the Catholic religion just seemed so complex and obscure. I responded by occasionally sending him blog posts, articles, and videos that did a good job explaining those aspects of Catholicism he was most curious about at the time.

You can also give your friend books to read. Several times I have worked with Protestants and brought books from home to drop off on their desk. Few people can resist a gift, so this tactic is a good way to get them reading something helpful. I would nonchalantly tell them that the book helped me learn my Faith better, or something very non-threatening like that, and invariably I got positive responses from it.

Remember that different lures work for different kinds of fish. Try one, and if it doesn't work, consider another one. If you hit brick wall after brick wall, turn your efforts to another friend who is more open to discussion.

RECOMMENDED READING
• *The Bible, New Revised Standard Version, Catholic Edition*
• *Catechism of the Catholic Church*

NAVIGATING
THE TIBER

PART I

SETTING SAIL

1

SURVEYING
THE DEPTHS

BEFORE WE CAN make more headway, we need to take a brief survey of the vast and varied landscape that is Protestantism. Doing so will allow you to mentally "place" your Protestant friend on the map and therefore understand how his beliefs generally cluster. While many similarities exist in Protestant beliefs, significant differences do as well, so it is important to acquaint yourself with the particular Protestant tradition of your friend.

A VAST OCEAN OF COMPETING BELIEFS

An older Catholic man who had read *The Protestant's Dilemma* told me how bewildered he was by all the different Protestant communities and what they believed:

> As a life-long Catholic who grew up in the 1950s, I am painfully aware that I was poorly catechized and even though I am presently in my mid-70s, decided that I would try to rectify this by reading about and learning my faith.
>
> I have tried very hard to find out exactly what the major denominations among our separated brethren really believe in order to better understand what these various Protestant denominations truly believe, but have just about given up due to frustration and becoming more confused than previously.

Before you engage any Protestant in dialogue, it's important to have at least a basic sense of where he's coming from. This is not to put strict labels on people—everyone has a story that is unique in some way. Nonetheless, most kinds of Protestants have beliefs that stem from a particular tradition, which informs their thinking whether they realize it fully or not. Knowing your friend's tradition will make your conversation more fruitful. Through many years of reading, discussion, and study, I've pieced together a pretty good survey of the seascape of Protestantism, which I will now share with you.

WE'RE ALL "OKAY"

When you reassure your friend that you believe him to be a Christian with the Holy Spirit living in his heart, be prepared for him to say "Great! You think I'm a Christian. I think you're a Christian, too—so why are we wasting time discussing all this?"

The best response is for you together to read John 17, where Jesus prays that all those whom the Father has given him will be perfectly one with each other. The fact is, you and your friend are not perfectly one. You believe different things on important issues; you worship at different churches that have no relationship with each other, and so by Christ's command you must both strive to overcome these divisions. We are not all okay. If God has established a visible Church with dogmas and rightfully appointed leaders, we all need to get in that Church. Remaining outside of it imperils our souls.

EVANGELICALS, SOUTHERN BAPTISTS, NONDENOMINATIONALS

These groups make up a significant percentage of Protestantism. They are characterized by a strong adherence to *sola scriptura*, a rejection of all sacraments, believer's baptism that is purely symbolic, and a lack of emphasis on the Lord's Supper. They usually believe that it's impossible to lose one's salvation (once saved, always saved).

Their services are non-liturgical, usually dominated by contemporary Christian praise music and long sermons that center on explaining passages from the Bible. Many retain the belief that only men should be pastors. Their church organization is congregational: each church community is self-governing and autonomous, even if it may be joined to a larger para-church group (e.g., the Southern Baptist Convention) or have satellite campuses (as with modern Protestant mega-churches).

Often simply called "Evangelicals," these Christians focus on the need for a conversion experience, daily personal prayer and Scripture reading, and the importance of being attentive to the Holy Spirit's movement in one's life. Sometimes this can go to an extreme and lead to *sanctified intuitionism*, whereby an Evangelical considers most of his thoughts to be from God. Hence, if someone comes up to you and says, "God told me to tell you something," it is likely he is an Evangelical.

For an Evangelical who believes that God speaks to him directly and frequently, it can be difficult to make him see that he is missing something and has errors in his beliefs. Since he has experienced God's work in his life, he is reluctant to even consider the possibility that his beliefs are not completely true.

To their credit, Evangelicals believe firmly in the inspiration and inerrancy of Scripture. Because they value Scripture highly, arguments concerning the canon give them serious pause, as do verse interpretations that run contrary to their own. Catholics also believe in the Scripture's inspiration and inerrancy—even if these concepts are defined a bit differently—so this forms a common ground and increases Evangelicals' respect for Catholicism.

PENTECOSTALS

The Pentecostal, or charismatic, movement began in the United States in the twentieth century, but their communities can now be found around the globe. They have made great inroads in Africa and Latin America (once a bastion of Catholicism).

Pentecostals emphasize the immediate, direct work of the Holy Spirit in the life of the individual Christian and in the ecclesial community. Many Pentecostals go so far as to say that the Holy Spirit's movement in one's life can at times trump even the words of Scripture. The Bible is still seen as vitally important, especially in the context of the Holy Spirit revealing insights as a Christian reads Scripture.

Pentecostal services are emotional and exciting. Allegedly prophetic utterances are possible and even common among some congregations. Speaking in tongues, being baptized in the Holy Spirit (not connected to traditional water baptism), and being "slain in the Spirit"—where one falls over in a kind of ecstasy, often due to the laying-on of others' hands—are accepted as normal.

Pentecostalism influences the general Evangelical Protestant population as well. Although it's usually toned down substantially during church services, it's not unusual to hear an Evangelical claim he has spoken in tongues or been slain in the Spirit. One Evangelical friend of mine even agreed that the Spirit might lead one to act in a way that goes contrary to Scripture, the idea being that the exigencies of the moment require dramatic action that would not normally be sanctioned. Pentecostalism has even affected Catholicism, especially in the Catholic charismatic movement of the 1960s through the 1990s.

With Pentecostals, be ready to emphasize the Catholic Church's teachings that the Holy Spirit is alive and well, moving hearts, working miracles, and giving people biblical gifts (healing, prophecy, etc.). Unlike many Protestant denominations, the Catholic Church does *not* claim that the Holy Spirit's miraculous works stopped at the death of the last apostle. With this, we can agree with Pentecostals and find common ground there.

CALVINISTS AND NEO-REFORMED

Calvinists are found in Reformed and Presbyterian communities. As opposed to Congregationalist Baptists, Calvinist churches are grouped together to form larger units—a presbyteral ecclesiology—and are not individually autonomous.[1] They base their theological system primarily on the work of John Calvin and his theological descendants. Calvinists emphasize *sola scriptura,* but also *sola fide* and a set of doctrinal propositions that form an allegedly consistent framework, informally identified by the acronym TULIP.

TULIP stands for: Total depravity (man and all his actions are sinful; he is unable to do anything untainted by selfish motives; God alone can act to elect and save him), Unconditional election (God before the creation of the world predestined some people to salvation, and nothing in them or that they can do, or not do, changes that; for those not predestined, there is nothing they can do to be saved), Limited atonement (Christ died only for the elect, those predestined to salvation, and not for the reprobate); Irresistible grace (those elected by God obtain salvation not by their own will but by the sovereign grace of God); and Perseverance of the saints (those people elected by God will persevere in faith, and when they die go to heaven).

Calvinist communities fall in the middle, liturgically speaking, between Catholics and "low church" Protestants like Baptists. Baptism and the Lord's Supper are important "ordinances" connected to Calvinist covenant theology, signs and seals of the covenant of grace. However, baptismal regeneration and Christ's Real Presence in the Eucharist (as defined by the Catholic Church) are rejected. Calvinists will

---

1. However many splits have occurred in these groups, and hundreds of separate Reformed denominations now exist worldwide.

baptize infants, however, differentiating them from Baptists and other Evangelicals.

Calvinists typically hold a high view of the Bible's inerrancy and inspiration. They take theology seriously, and this is always an advantage when entering discussions with them. Apathy is rare. They know what they believe, and they believe they are right. Many verses can be plausibly interpreted to support the TULIP system, lending it credibility.

One main problem with Calvinist theology is its unbalanced focus on the omnipotence of God at the expense of man's free will. Catholics can actually agree with much of TULIP, amazingly enough, but not with all of it.[2] I've found it's best with Calvinists to skip the verse-wrangling and put the question of the canon of Scripture front and center. It undercuts their basis for arguing, since it challenges their ability to even know what books make up the Bible.

Reformed theology is, like Pentecostalism, crossing over Protestant boundaries and influencing Baptists and other Evangelicals. Many such traditional Protestants are retreating to the Reformed fort in an attempt to stave off the theological and moral liberalism that has been moving through Protestant denominations over the past century. Some Baptist churches are tacking on "Reformed" to the beginning of their names, and affirming that doctrine is important, systematic theology matters, and the consequences of God's sovereignty must not be watered down to make them more palatable to people. This Calvinist resurgence has also led to new groups called the Neo-Reformed. John Piper, a Reformed Baptist pastor, is emblematic of this new Calvinist movement.

---

2. Jimmy Akin has a high-level explanation of how much of TULIP Catholics can accept called A Tiptoe through TULIP: http://www.ewtn.com/library/ANSWERS/TULIP.htm.

LUTHERANS

Although Calvinists are perhaps the most purely "Protestant" Protestants, Lutherans came first and generally have better senses of humor. These denominations take after their respective founder's personality. Calvin was a lawyer, precise and exacting. Hence his rigorous theological system. Luther was an Augustinian friar, a priest. He drank beer, had big opinions, and retained many Catholic beliefs. Nonetheless, he was in many ways the original founder of Protestantism.

Lutherans focus on *sola fide,* but connect it directly with baptism. They affirm a doctrine similar to baptismal regeneration, and are therefore closer to Catholics than other Protestants. Their church services are liturgical. They have bishops and priests (also called pastors or reverends). They place heavy emphasis on baptism and the Lord's Supper. They have a belief in the Eucharist called sacramental union that is closer to the Real Presence than any other Protestant group's theology.

Luther himself retained strong faith in the Marian dogmas and thought that the early Church's Tradition was an indispensable treasure in understanding Scripture and properly interpreting it. And so, even as Lutherans affirm *sola scriptura,* they do not exclude all influence from Tradition.

Few Lutherans hold consistently to all that Luther taught. However, it is still valuable to present to them Luther's peculiar beliefs and ask them why they do or don't accept them. Especially with the Marian dogmas this is an interesting line to explore, as it gets to the root of what authority they are accepting.

LIBERALS

Liberal Protestants are found in varying concentrations in every Protestant denomination. Many splits in Protestantism have been caused when a liberal group got the majority and began changing their church's doctrine, causing traditional members to break away in order to protect themselves from the changes, often only to see the same thing happen again in a few decades' time. So, for example, the Presbyterian Church USA is generally liberal, whereas the Presbyterian Church in America is generally traditional, and the Orthodox Presbyterian Church is even more traditional. Similarly the Evangelical Lutheran Church in America is liberal on average, while the Lutheran Church Missouri Synod is traditional and the Wisconsin Synod even more so.

Liberal Protestants generally reject the inspiration and inerrancy of Scripture. They bought into the historical-critical method of analyzing the Bible that claimed to discover the "true" meaning of the Bible. This method had its origins in the Reformation itself, and subsequently the rationalism of the Enlightenment. Ancient truths were discarded and novelties were adopted. As such, liberal Protestants decided that many traditional Christian doctrines are culturally conditional and therefore reversible. Many liberal Protestants accept women pastors and same-sex relationships, and some reject core tenets of Christianity, such as belief in the Resurrection and the divinity of Christ.

Engaging liberal Protestants in a discussion is often an exercise in frustration and futility. Because they do not hold to traditional Christian teachings or even believe in the authority of Scripture, there's less common ground on which to build. And their wide range of beliefs (or disbeliefs) make them moving targets. Nonetheless, since they generally profess to value tolerance and open-mindedness, they can also be more agreeable to hearing your ideas and reading books you suggest.

Nail down your liberal Protestant friend on the existence of objective truth. Before you can make any progress, he must be willing to see that truth is not relative. Jesus claimed to be God, so he couldn't just be a guru-like teacher: either he was a liar, a madman, or the Son of God. You can also try bringing up moral questions to get him to admit objective truth exists: rape isn't morally relative, for example. Once you have at least a reluctant agreement that truth exists you can move forward.

ANGLICANS, METHODISTS, AND QUAKERS

These groups all owe their origin to the English Reformation, instigated in the sixteenth century by King Henry VIII's desire to divorce his wife, Catherine of Aragon, and subsequent declaration of himself as head of the Church in England. This break with Rome led to the (often violent) dissolution of English Catholicism and, later, further divisions within English Protestantism.

Anglicans belong to the Church of England, also called the Anglican Communion, which is a worldwide Protestant community. Episcopalians are the U.S. branch of Anglicanism. The interesting thing about Anglicans is that they preserved Catholicism's clerical hierarchy, with the archbishop of Canterbury as the titular head—though his authority is not analogous to the pope's, nor does anyone believe him to be infallible. In spite of the similar clerical structure, the Catholic Church does not recognize Anglicans as having a valid sacrament of holy orders. In several ways they broke the chain of apostolic succession required for valid ordinations. Nonetheless, many Anglican priests—even married ones—become Catholic, and some become Catholic priests after a period of formation.

Anglicanism is firmly Protestant; however, many of its adherents distance themselves from the label, instead claiming they are a "middle way" between Catholicism and Protestantism. They also maintain that they are an "apostolic" Church and desire to be placed alongside Eastern Orthodoxy and Catholicism. However, historically and theologically they are Protestant, in spite of their Catholic-like ecclesiology and the fact that their beginnings included validly ordained Catholic bishops who bowed to King Henry VIII and broke in schism from the Catholic Church. Influenced by Lutheran and Calvinist ideas, the Anglicans ended up with something of their own unique theology, albeit substantially similar on most issues to that of the magisterial Reformers.

Their liturgy is very similar to the Catholic Church's. Even so, both "high church" and "low church" Anglicans exist, those who identify more with Evangelical Protestantism and those, sometimes called Anglo-Catholics, who lean closer to Catholicism. They are all supposed to get along under the "big tent" of Anglicanism, but in recent decades fissures have developed between the more traditional Anglicans (now often found in Africa) and the liberal ones (who dominate the Episcopal Church in the United States). Divisions have formed over women's episcopal ordination and the ordination of persons with same-sex attraction.

Pope Benedict XVI created the Anglican Ordinariate as a way for traditional Anglicans to become Catholic while retaining the authentic aspects of their spiritual patrimony, and many Anglicans are now crossing over the Tiber via that bridge. (If you have an Anglican Ordinariate parish in your area, I highly recommend you go and visit it. The liturgy is quite beautiful and reverent.)

Methodists are an eighteenth-century offshoot from Anglicanism, with John Wesley founding what was for the most part an amicable split from his mother denomination. Methodism grew especially through revivals, first in England, then in the United States. Methodists emphasize four "sources" to decide theological matters: Scripture, Tradition, Reason, and

Experience, with Scripture having the primary position.

Wesley was influenced by the pietistic movement that focused on personal piety and living a faithful Christian life, and this hallmark is seen in many Methodists today. However, liberalism has heavily influenced Methodism in the United States, so if you meet a Methodist it's best to carefully inquire into his beliefs instead of assuming you already know what they are.

Like Methodists, Quakers (Society of Friends) are an offshoot of the Anglican Communion. They emphasize a personal experience with Christ and a deeply devotional life. Quakers have been influenced by many different Protestant movements, and today several distinct groups exist, the three most representative of which are: Evangelical Quakers who are similar theologically to other Evangelical Protestants; Gurneyite Friends, who are generally Protestant while retaining some degree of "unprogrammed worship," where there is no pastor or leader but members who sit silently until the Holy Spirit prompts one of them to say something to the rest of the congregation; Liberal, Universalist, and Non-theist Friends who range on the theological spectrum from liberal Protestantism to completely non-Christian.

ANABAPTISTS, MENNONITES, AMISH

Anabaptists (literally "re-baptizers") were the fourth reforming movement of the Protestant Reformation. Their origins are still debated, but early on in the Reformation they appeared and their hallmarks were a rejection of infant baptism—hence their name, as they would re-baptize converts—and an aversion to oaths and being involved in civil government. They believe in *sola scriptura*, the priesthood of all believers, and are usually pacifists.

The Mennonites and their nephew, the Amish, are Anabaptists. They associate in close communities, often dress in an old-fashioned way, and are known to reject technological or industrial machines that would weaken the interdependent ties from person to person in their community. In varying degrees, all Mennonites and Amish follow the Anabaptist principle of separation from the world.

CHURCHES OF CHRIST AND DISCIPLES OF CHRIST

The Churches of Christ and the Disciples of Christ formed in the nineteenth century, during what is known as the Restoration Movement in American Protestantism. Their goal was to return to primitive, apostolic Christianity, which they believed they understood from reading the New Testament. These groups reject being called Protestants and do not think they are a denomination, but rather the true expression of apostolic Christianity as it was practiced in the first century.

In reality they are firmly Protestant in their beliefs and form a denomination—one that has now split multiple times like most others in Protestantism—but they will not concede this. Interestingly, they are strict in requiring (believer's) baptism for salvation and weekly church attendance on Sundays to observe the Lord's Supper. In this respect they are closer to Catholicism, although their beliefs fall short of Catholic sacramentalism. They are Congregationalists and have no denominational structure.

EMERGENT AND HIPSTERS

This is a relatively new group within Protestantism, a movement that has affected many denominations but also boasts churches in its own right. Emergent Christians are often liberal in their theology, but some more traditional Evangelicals have fled the culture-war politics of American Evangelicalism to join Emergent churches. Many of these hipster Christians were burned in one way or another in more traditional church-es and want a place to be "free" and worship God as they like.

Emergent and hipster Christians are willing to combine elements of other denominations, often creating their own liturgical services. On any given Sunday at an Emergent church, you might find people painting, singing, dancing, or doing skits, even during the service itself. One church that my Protestant (now Catholic!) friend went to was called Mosaic and was formed by Baptists, but their liturgy was a custom creation based on the Anglican Book of Common Prayer. (That Mosaic church ended up shutting down, but then another, non-related Protestant church sprang up in the same city and called itself Mosaic. It is an irresistible name for Protestants, I suppose.)

Many Emergent Christians don't like being labeled as such, and it's impossible to know what one believes without careful questioning. Generally they are not quite certain what they believe—that's why they're going to an Emergent church—but this is an opportunity to help them see that the truth can be known and is found in the Catholic Church.

WHERE TO BEGIN?

Now that you have an idea of the vast Protestant landscape, it's time to begin your discussion. Though Protestants differ greatly, their common beliefs allow us to choose the most important topics to tackle first. And that is what we will do. From there, we will roll with the ship as it rocks back and forth along the currents of your conversation, finding the best places to put into harbor at each stop.

RECOMMENDED READING
Handbook of Denominations in the United States, by Craig D. Atwood

2

IN THE BEGINNING WAS THE CANON

You could begin the discussion with your friend at many different points, but the one that makes the most sense is the *canon of Scripture*. The canon is the set of books that make up the Bible—the "table of contents" of Scripture—and it is one of the most important issues between Catholics and Protestants for two reasons: first, because the Catholic and Protestant canons differ (Catholics have seventy-three books in their canon while Protestants have sixty-six), and second, because Protestants believe in a doctrine called *sola scriptura*, or "the Bible alone."

WHICH BOOKS MAKE UP THE BIBLE?

Sola scriptura means that the Bible is the sole source of public revelation given by God to man and the sole inerrant rule of faith. This is one of the two core doctrines of Protestantism (the other being *sola fide*, or "faith alone," which we will encounter later), and so it presents an excellent starting point for your discussion. For Scripture to be the sole rule of faith, it stands to reason that we must first know which books, exactly, make up Scripture (i.e., the biblical canon). A further requirement is that we know this biblical canon with a certainty strong enough to bind our consciences. After all, if we believe that God inspired authoritative, inerrant books to be written, but we don't know how to tell those books apart from non-authoritative books of merely human origin, then we are left without any rule of faith we can follow with confidence

The first thing you will need to make clear when speaking with your friend is that you are talking about the Bible's *table of contents* and not the content of the Bible's books. This simple point can be hard for many Protestants to understand because most of them have given little thought as to why the particular sixty-six books in their Bibles are the right ones. They were given Protestant Bibles when they were young and implicitly accepted as inspired all the books it included (and no others). It may even be helpful to have them open up to the beginning of their Bibles and look at the table of contents page itself, which is usually broken up into an Old Testament section and a New Testament section.

Once you are both on the same page about the fact that you are discussing the canon, begin by asking your friend why he accepts those particular books as being inspired. He may or may not have an answer, and if he doesn't, that's okay. Give him an "action item" to research it and come back to you with an answer at your next meeting. Then again, he may reply that he knows those books are true because he has read them and tried to live by them, and he has felt the grace of God through the words. This is a popular answer, and although it's ultimately not good enough to satisfy the requirement for knowing the canon, there is some truth to it: God *does* give us grace through the inspired words of the Bible. But using this as the primary criterion for knowing the canon is similar to the "burning in the bosom" that Mormons claim they feel when they read the Book of Mormon, proving that it is "another testament of Jesus Christ." So you can then ask your friend how he knows that what he feels in his heart is from God, but a Mormon's bosom-burning is not. This is a pow-

WHAT'S GOOD ABOUT PROTESTANTISM?

Protestantism has a number of positive aspects, beginning with the Protestant Christians themselves.

1. Protestants love Jesus. They believe in him with all their hearts and desire to know him, follow him, and become more like him. Their single-minded devotion to Christ is admirable and sets a great example for us as Catholics.

2. Protestants love the Bible. They believe that it is God's word and read it often. They memorize Scripture verses. They constantly do Bible studies on particular books to understand them better. Unfortunately, having divorced the Scriptures from Christ's Church, these Bible studies often contain many errors, but at least the intention in having them is noble.

3. Protestants are great evangelizers. This is the area where Protestants often put Catholics to shame. Protestants love to evangelize, to share the gospel of Christ. They have found life in Christ and desire that others share the joy of living in the freedom that only Jesus brings, the freedom of living in the truth.

erful argument because almost all Protestants do not believe that Mormons are Christians, so they rightfully feel uncomfortable using a Mormon rationale as their own.

Your friend may also candidly admit that he accepted the Bible given to him by his parents (or pastor or friend) and that he had never questioned why it contained those particular sixty-six books. Such an answer is rare and demonstrates a laudable openness to discovering the truth, an invaluable quality for the kind of discussion that you wish to have. In this case, you can proceed to explain why the Catholic position on the canon is solid while the Protestant one is not (see below).

But let's say that your friend is better prepared, or that you meet with him again after has done some studying on the history of the canon. He may confidently tell you that the Protestant canon is the true one because it was accepted from the very beginning by the early Christians. Now, this claim is false, but it is repeated in enough Protestant books and websites that your friend cannot be faulted for assuming it was true. Without going into more depth on the history of the canon—we will do this later on—let him know that the early Church did *not* universally agree on the canon of Scripture or even realize it was something that was an immediate necessity. The simple fact is that while some books were widely accepted in the first fifty to 100 years of the Church, many others were disputed up through the second, third, and even fourth centuries.

If your friend doubts this claim, give him these facts for his consideration and further study for your next visit.

1. If acceptance of the canon were universal early on, you would expect all Christian groups to agree on one canon; but the Catholic canon has seventy-three books, not sixty-six. And the Eastern Orthodox, who broke in schism from the Catholic Church in A.D. 1054, have an even different canon, with seventy-five books.

2. Martin Luther himself, the central figure who started the Protestant Reformation, doubted the canonicity of four books of the New Testament because, in part, they were *not* universally accepted in the early Church.

3. It was not until A.D. 367 that St. Athanasius, a bishop in the early Church, unambiguously proposed the exact list of twenty-seven books that all Christians now accept as the New Testament. Before that time, many conflicting lists had been created, some including spurious books and others excluding genuine ones.

All this historical evidence is against the claim that the canon was known from the beginning of the Church.

CATHOLICISM'S CONSISTENT CANON

So what is the Catholic position on the canon and why is it stronger than the Protestant one? The Catholic Church teaches that God has protected it from error in all its dogmatic teachings on faith and morals, and since the canon of Scripture falls under the "faith" category, a Catholic can know that the Church's canon is inerrant. This may at first not seem any stronger than the Protestant position because the Catholic Church's claim of divine protection from error may itself be false, but the fact that both positions *may* be false does not mean that one is not stronger or more reasonable than the other.

Consider that Protestants believe that God protected only one thing from error—the contents of the Bible's books—whereas Catholics believe that he protected those books from error along with the *canon that lists those books*, and you can see that the Catholic teaching is consistent while the Protestant teaching is *ad hoc*. It is not based on a principled reason for believing that God protected the Church from error on one thing but not on another. It would not help if a Protestant were to say, "I also believe that God protected the canon from error *in addition to* the contents of the biblical books," because it is still *ad hoc* to believe God protected *two* things from error instead of just one thing.

Both Catholics and Protestants can offer pieces of historical data to support the particular books in their respective canons, but mere data can never give certainty that God protected any canon from error. The data do not point to *any* one canon without ambiguity or controversy, and the early Christians who wrote about the books they considered inspired gave conflicting lists for 400 years. Without a rock-solid foundation for believing that God protected someone from erring when discerning the canon, Protestants are left believing that the Bible is the sole infallible rule of faith while not having certainty in what books make up that Bible. This conundrum led a well-known Protestant pastor named R.C. Sproul to admit that the Bible is a "fallible collection of infallible books."[3]

If you find that statement confusing, you are not alone. How can we know that a book's contents are inerrant if we don't know for sure that it is an inerrant book? This makes no sense, yet countless Protestants repeat Sproul's answer when faced with the canon question.

Surely, refuting the Protestant position on the canon cannot be that simple? In fact, it can be, and it is. However, it will take time for your Protestant friend to comprehend these arguments—not because he is dim-witted or lacks faith, but because he has been steeped in a set of Protestant traditions that form the fundamental basis for his beliefs, and such things aren't discarded in an instant. However, he does not have to be convinced just from this one argument. In the next chapter we will look at the next weak link in Protestantism's armor: the "*sola*" part of *sola scriptura*.

YOUR PRAYER TOGETHER

"Dear Lord, we thank you for the time you have brought us together today to discuss these important topics. Our desire is for you, to know you in spirit and in truth. Lead us to Christ and His truth. In Jesus' Name we pray, amen."

RECOMMENDED READING

The Protestant's Dilemma, by Devin Rose

---

3. R.C. Sproul, *Now That's a Good Question!* (Nelson, 1996), p. 81-82.

3

THE BIBLE *ALONE?*

THE FUNDAMENTAL PROTESTANT doctrine, *sola scriptura*, has two weak links. We already showed the key problem behind the *scriptura* part—that of the canon—and now we look at the second weak link: the *sola* part.

Very simply, your Protestant friend must demonstrate how he knows that the Bible *alone* is the sole rule of faith, the sole repository of divine revelation, the one thing that can be trusted to communicate to us supernatural truth. For this part of the discussion, you can "spot" him the canon, that is, you can let him assume that his belief that the Bible contains sixty-six books is correct.

A *SOLA SCRIPTURA* PROOFTEXT?

Ask him directly: "Why do you believe that the Bible is the sole rule of faith?" You will likely get one of a few different answers.

The first argument to expect is a quote from 2 Timothy 3:16-17: "All scripture is inspired by God and is useful for teaching, for reproof, for correction, and for training in righteousness, so that everyone who belongs to God may be proficient, equipped for every good work." Your friend will have been taught to interpret these verses as saying that the Bible is the sole rule of faith, since it equips Christians for "every good work." Some translations add that it makes Christians "complete."

This interpretation stretches these verses beyond St. Paul's meaning. Catholics can certainly agree that all Scripture is inspired by God (even as we disagree on which books make up Scripture). And Catholics can happily agree that Scripture is useful for teaching, reproof, correction, and training in righteousness. Further, when used properly, Scripture equips God's people for every good work. In other words, Catholics can agree with this passage in its entirety.

Although Protestants have been trained to read the Bible and apply each passage to themselves in an individualistic way, that is not always the proper way to interpret it. For instance, you should remind your friend that this letter—2 Timothy—was written from one teacher, Paul, to another one, Timothy. Both men were teachers and rightful leaders in the early Church. As such, Paul's primary purpose in this passage is explaining to Timothy as a teacher of the Faith how he can use the Bible to equip the members of his flock. Through Timothy's reliable instruction from Scripture,

WHAT IF YOU GET STUMPED?

At some point in your dialogue, your friend will ask you a question or present an argument that you will not know how to respond to. Don't be alarmed! Part of what makes having a discussion like this one profitable is being willing to learn and grow yourself.

When this situation occurs, tell your friend that you need time to think about what he said and research it more. Then do an online search for the topic or look in the *Catechism*. Otherwise, consult a trusted friend or priest.

Have confidence in Christ and his Church. There is no question that does not have a good answer, nor argument that can "break" the Church. This is because God established it (and not because Catholics are any smarter or more faithful than others).

Above all, remember the Golden Rule here: when you stump him, give him the time and space to investigate your claims more fully, just as you would expect that leeway from him if the shoe were on the other foot.

the people of God under his care will be equipped for every good work, and he will be able to offer them reproof, correction, and training—all things that a teacher provides his disciples.

Furthermore, the "Scripture" about which Paul is writing to Timothy is the Old Testament, which he had learned growing up. Some books of the New Testament hadn't even been written yet, and the canon was still a long way away from being decided. So if this verse proves *sola scriptura*, it proves too much, because the Old Testament alone would then be the sole infallible rule of faith! Now, read to your friend the verses just prior to these: "But as for you, continue in what you have learned and have become convinced of, because you know those from whom you learned it, and how from infancy you have known the Holy Scriptures, which are able to make you wise for salvation through faith in Christ Jesus" (2 Tim. 3:14-15). Note first how he talks to Timothy of Scripture he knew "from infancy," confirming that he's talking about the Old Testament. Second, Paul exhorts Timothy to hold fast to what he had been taught by Paul himself, knowing that the apostle's teachings were true. This is not an appeal Scripture alone, but rather to Scripture and the Apostolic Tradition.

PLANTING THE SEED OF TRADITION

Here you might follow up by mentioning that elsewhere in the Bible Paul also tells Christians to hold fast to apostolic teachings that came not just by letter (like the epistles of the New Testament) but by word of mouth. (2 Thess. 2:15, 3:6). He might say that those oral teachings eventually became part of Scripture, but we have no reason to believe that *all* of apostolic Tradition was "crystallized" in the relatively few letters of the New Testament. Only if you first assume *sola scriptura* to be true are you forced into this conclusion.

Finally, we find an interesting verse in the previous letter of Paul to Timothy that is relevant to this question: "But if I should be delayed, you should know how to behave in the household of God, which is the church of the living God, the pillar and foundation of truth" (1 Tim. 3:15). Here the Church is spoken of in exalted terms for its support of the truth of God. If we used this verse out of context, as many Protestants use 2 Timothy 3:16-17, we might conclude that *the Church* is the sole infallible rule of faith!

Only when we take the Bible as a whole do we see that Scripture, Tradition, and the Church are integral to knowing and understanding divine revelation. Authority is not held up by the one leg of Scripture alone; it's a three-legged stool, held up by the Bible, Sacred Tradition, and the teaching authority (Magisterium) of the Church. You can show your friend an example of that teaching authority in the Bible, where in Acts 15 the apostles and their disciples interpreted revelation and made binding decisions upon all Christians (in what came to be known as the Council of Jerusalem). That same teaching authority is living today in the Catholic Church, whose teachers—the bishops—are in direct succession from the apostles themselves, just as Timothy and Titus succeeded Paul and other qualified men succeeded them.

"EVERYTHING BUT SCRIPTURE IS CORRUPTED"

A second argument your friend might give in favor of *sola scriptura* is the "corruption" argument. The theory goes that anything not written down will become corrupted over time, kind of like a big game of Telephone, where one person whispers something to another and so on until the final message is garbled beyond recognition. Therefore, nothing but the written word of the Bible can be trusted as uncorrupted.

In response, you can offer your friend two factors that

demonstrate why it is plausible to believe that Sacred Tradition is trustworthy. First, the Holy Spirit can protect the integrity of oral tradition just as we believe He protected the integrity of written Scripture. This isn't proof that Sacred Tradition is in fact protected by the Holy Spirit, but your friend has to admit that he at least recognizes the principle. If God can inspire Scripture in order to make his revelation known correctly, why can't he give a similar charism to another type of transmission of that revelation? The Holy Spirit can protect Tradition from error as easily as he does Scripture. So the question isn't *whether* God could protect something other than the Bible from corruption—he certainly could—but *how* exactly we know what he protected from error and what he did not.

Second, because the divine revelation entrusted to the apostles and by them to their successors was something so important to them, something they had to fight to protect and defend, they would not let falsehood corrupt it. Right from the beginning of the Church men invented false teachings—or twisted the true teachings—and sought to win approval for their heretical ideas. And so the leaders of the Church—the bishops and priests—had to carefully understand and forcefully defend the Faith against errors. When the early Christians wrote treatises against heretics, they appealed to the Tradition handed down to them by the apostles and their successors as well as to Sacred Scripture. Most heretics were well-versed in Scripture and tried to use it to further their own ideas.

In fact, the early Christians argued that scriptural interpretations put forward by heretics were counter to the interpretation given to them through apostolic Tradition, and that's how they knew those teachings were false. The early Church believed Tradition to be reliable.

St. Irenaeus wrote against heretics in the second century, testifying to the Church's Tradition that stemmed directly from the succession that the bishops of the Church were given from the apostles themselves:

> "In this order, and by this succession, the ecclesiastical tradition from the apostles, and the preaching of the truth, have come down to us. And this is most abundant proof that there is one and the same vivifying faith, which has been preserved in the Church from the apostles until now, and handed in truth." *Against Heresies* 3, 3, 3

When those heretics put forward wrong interpretations of Scripture and tried to claim that they had their own tradition that was the true one, Irenaeus refuted them from the authority of Scripture and Tradition:

> "But, again, when we refer them to that tradition which originates from the apostles, [and] which is preserved by means of the succession of presbyters in the Churches, they object to tradition, saying that they themselves are wiser not merely than the presbyters, but even than the apostles, because they have discovered the unadulterated truth. . . . It comes to this, therefore, that these men do now consent neither to Scripture nor to tradition." *Against Heresies* 3, 2, 2

Tellingly, St. Irenaeus drew from both Tradition and Scripture to demonstrate that the heretics were not from God. They were following their own interpretation of the Bible and falling into grave errors, not unlike Protestants have done.

BOOTSTRAPPING THE BIBLE?

To close this discussion, another question to pose to your friend runs like this: How was the early Church supposed to base itself on the Bible alone when the Bible hadn't been completely written until late in the first century? How, for that matter, was the Church in the second, third, and fourth centuries supposed to function with *sola scriptura* when the canon of books that make up the Bible was still being finalized? Not to mention, written works in those early centuries were scarce. Most—nearly all—early Christians did not have personal access to the books of the Bible. What rule of faith did they follow?

Present these arguments to your friend and ask him how he can say that the Bible *alone* is the sole infallible rule of faith and deposit of revelation. Give him time to process this information and allow him space to do more research if he wants to. *Sola scriptura* is a doctrine he no doubt accepted early on in his life of faith, and he will not relinquish it easily. To let go of it is to admit that Protestantism is wrong on one of its two fundamental doctrines, a disturbing thought, at least initially, for any Protestant.

YOUR PRAYER TOGETHER
"God of love and truth, continue to draw us deeper into your heart, that we may know how best to follow you wherever you lead. In Christ's Name we pray, amen."

RECOMMENDED READING
101 Biblical Arguments Against Sola Scriptura, by Dave Armstrong

4

APOSTOLIC
SUCCESSION AND
TRADITION

As you are already demonstrating to your friend, the Bible is not alone; it is accompanied by apostolic succession and Tradition within the embrace of the Church. Inevitably, ecumenical discussions return to what the God-given source of divine revelation is. Protestants say the Bible alone is that source. The Catholic Church says the source is Scripture and Tradition. How one answers this question determines whether one joins the Catholic Church or remains Protestant. A non-*sola scriptura* Protestant is an oxymoron, although some do exist; and a "Catholic" who rejects the Apostolic Tradition has a serious moral dilemma, since the Church binds his conscience to believe in it. How can we figure out which is true?

We have several possible approaches. First is the canon of Scripture itself, which requires some tradition outside of Scripture to know. This is evident because nowhere in the books of Scripture is the table of contents for the Bible found. Further, imagine the case where we start with zero books of Scripture—we have not yet discerned any are inspired—and we want to figure out the canon. But how do we start? Maybe your friend would say, surely you can start with Genesis and Exodus, since the Jewish people universally accepted those as inspired. And for the New Testament you could start with Matthew and Luke, since those received widespread early adoption. But realize that in doing this "bootstrapping," we are accepting the decisions made by various persons, none of whom Protestants believe were infallibly protected from error by God in their discernment. Perhaps the Jews made a mistake, and similarly the early Christians? Since Protestants do not trust the Tradition used by these Christians to discern the books of the New Testament, they cannot accept the decision made under its influence.

Another approach to determining whether apostolic succession and Tradition are of divine origin is to start with the early Church. St. Paul tells St. Timothy: "What you have heard from me before many witnesses entrust to faithful men who will be able to teach others also" (2 Tim. 2:2). Read the writings of St. Clement in the first century, St. Ignatius of Antioch in the early 100s, St. Justin Martyr and St. Irenaeus later on in the second century, and you will get a good idea of how the early Church viewed itself with regard to the deposit of faith and the rightful leadership of the Church. Namely, that God established rightful authority in His Church, beginning with the apostles and continuing to the men whom they ordained.

Invite your Protestant friend to join you in this reading. A good book study to do together would be Rod Bennett's *The Four Witnesses*.[4] You could also read relevant passages from these Fathers' writings online.[5] It will quickly be established that the early Church recognized that there were rightful leaders of the Church and false ones, and that the latter sought to wrest authority from the former. We see this conflict already

4. Published by Ignatius Press in 2002 and available online or in Catholic bookstores.
5. To find these passages read the Catholic Answers' article here: http://www.catholic.com/tracts/apostolic-succession.

in 3 John where the apostle calls out Diotrephes and informs the flock that he will personally come there very soon and set this usurper in his place. Similarly, the rightful leaders of Christ's Church had succession from the apostles via the laying on of hands. God knew that the apostles would one day all die, but he didn't leave his Church alone: He established apostolic succession to ensure his Church had leaders.

But what would happen, your friend may ask, when these leaders went astray, morally or doctrinally? This is where apostolic Tradition comes in. This is the Church's Tradition, and it is inseparably connected to succession itself. Tradition is the living river of life that springs from Christ and flows within the Church down through the ages to our present day. The Holy Spirit enlivens it and guides its flow. So even when individual bishops and priests have acted immorally or personally accepted heresy, the Spirit has prevented their errors from corrupting the teachings of the Church. Hence, we can have confidence that the Church's doctrine on faith and morals is true. This Tradition is attested to by St. Irenaeus powerfully, even as he praises Scripture and its privileged place in the Church. He saw no conflict between apostolic succession, Tradition, and Scripture. Rather, they functioned together like vital organs in a body. That body is the Church, Christ's mystical Body, of which he is the head.

With this strong historical witness, even from the earliest times, to apostolic succession and Tradition, your Protestant friend is faced with a now-familiar dilemma: either the Church went off the rails shortly after Christ established her, or his Protestant beliefs contain serious errors. Clearly, he would rather believe the former to be true. But that places him, in this respect, right alongside Mormons, who claim that a great apostasy occurred within a century of the death of the apostles. The Church fell into error and is thus untrustworthy.

Accepting such a situation leads to other insurmountable difficulties, like the inability to accept the canon that this same corrupted early Church discerned. It leads many Protestants to "go liberal" and reject the belief in the inspiration of Scripture altogether. That's too bad, because the better alternative is not to take a step backward, away from faith, but to take a step forward in faith and accept *all* that God has done for the world through his Church.

Even if a Protestant continues to reject apostolic Tradition, the fact remains that he accepts some other tradition, as evidenced by the lens through which he interprets Scripture, the basis for which he accepts the sixty-six–book Protestant canon, the key verses through which he interprets others. This tradition is usually informed by his upbringing, certain Reformers (whether Luther, Calvin, Zwingli, the Anglicans, or the Anabaptists), his current ecclesial community, its pastor, his friends, and the books he reads. In the absence of Sacred Tradition, he's created his own human tradition instead. And if Protestantism is true, other people must do the same as he and come up with their own tradition, unique no doubt from all the others but with no authority or power to bind the conscience of anyone else.

YOUR PRAYER TOGETHER
The Apostles' Creed.

RECOMMENDED READING
The Meaning of Tradition, by Yves Congar, O.P.

5

FAITH *ALONE?*

WE DISCUSSED THE first plank of the Reformation—*sola scriptura*—and now it's time to tackle the second: *sola fide,* or "justification through faith alone."

Interestingly, justification is less important today in most Protestants' minds than it was during the time of the Reformation. In some conversations, the topic will not even come up. But, if you are engaging a Reformed Protestant, Lutheran, or serious Evangelical in your dialogue, you can be almost guaranteed that he will bring it up. That's good—it gives you a chance to educate them on the Catholic position.

TWO THEORIES OF SALVATION

Justification is the process whereby a person becomes righteous before God. Sin makes us unrighteous. Only Jesus Christ can make us righteous again. Catholics and Protestants both agree on this. The sticking points come when we ask *how,* exactly, Christ makes us righteous, what (if anything) it takes on our part to become righteous, and whether justification is a onetime event or also includes an ongoing aspect.

The first obstacle to demonstrating the reasonableness of the Catholic doctrines on justification is that Protestants and Catholics have imbued the word with different meanings. For Protestants, justification means a *onetime event* wherein someone who is unjustified becomes justified—made savable in God's eyes. For Catholics, justification includes this event,

WHEN THE TOME COMES OUT
I was about to have another lunch conversation with Cal, a Presbyterian with Evangelical leanings (meaning that, for instance, he rejected infant baptism but followed most of John Calvin's other teachings).

I had gotten him on the ropes with the arguments presented in the chapters on the canon, but he had gone to his arsenal and come ready this time. He pulled out a dense textbook on systematic theology by a Reformed Protestant scholar and laid it on the table. If something like this happens to you, do not be alarmed. There are no killer arguments that can sink Catholicism—not because we Catholics are so smart, but simply because the Catholic Church is true and Christ has guided it into all truth.

We began our talk on justification by reading through the first chapters of Romans. Here is where having a solid Catholic study Bible will again prove indispensable. Get the Ignatius New Testament Study Bible. Its notes are orthodox and were crafted knowing the common Protestant arguments against the Catholic Church's doctrines. Prep for the conversation by reading

but also an ongoing process in which the Christian grows in righteousness. Protestants call that ongoing process *sanctification* and consider it separate from justification.

Explain this difference in definition to your Protestant friend and do not move on until he has acknowledged its existence. It is not necessary to agree on a definition at this time—it is enough to simply realize that the disparity exists.

The second obstacle to achieving mutual understanding is the difference between the Catholic conception of grace and atonement and the Protestant one. Catholics believe that before the fall of man, Adam and Eve were in friendship with God. The sin they committed caused the loss of that friendship, the loss of what we call *sanctifying grace*. Jesus Christ, through his death and resurrection, reconciled us to God through his perfect offering of love to the Father. Jesus therefore made it possible for us to return to the state of friendship with God. Catholics believe this occurs by grace, through faith, beginning with the sacrament of baptism. (Notice that I did not say through faith *alone*. More will be said of that momentarily.)

the chapter and accompanying notes ahead of time.

My discussion with Cal followed the lines of argument I present here in justification.

Protestants, on the other hand, believe that at the fall human beings did not just lose friendship with God and become prone to sin, but became fundamentally corrupted. Since even one sin separates us from God, we deserve hell for even one sin we commit. The cosmic problem faced by man before the Incarnation was that he could never fulfill God's law perfectly and thus could never be righteous in God's sight. So God sent Jesus, who lived a perfect life of obedience to the Father. Protestants contend that we deserved God's wrath, but Jesus willingly took our place and endured the punishment for our sins. This idea is called *penal substitution*. Now, Protestantism alleges, we could be justified by grace through faith alone. When we put our faith in Jesus, God no longer reckons our sins to us but instead imputes Christ's righteousness to us.

It's as if God looks at us only through Christ, so that even though we are still sinful and wicked, God doesn't see that but only sees his Son's perfect righteousness. Another way this is sometimes explained is that we owed an infinite amount of money that we could never pay, but when we put our faith in Jesus, he credits an infinite amount of money into our bank account so we can pay the debt.

This is complicated, and brilliant men and women have pondered these different ideas for centuries. However, the purpose here is for you to understand the basic shape of Catholic and Protestant theologies surrounding justification. Protestantism's conception of God's wrath and imputed righteousness is problematic, but with most Protestants it is not worth delving deeply into this particular aspect of their beliefs.[6] They learned it from their pastor, from their Bible's study notes, from their parents and friends.

If you do think it worthwhile to delve into this further in your particular conversation, start with this thought experiment: if Protestantism were true, God the Father would have done something evil by pouring out his wrath upon an innocent man (Jesus). Bryan Cross explained this Protestant dilemma in regard to the atonement:

> If God the Father was pouring out his wrath on the Second Person of the Trinity, then God was divided against himself, God the Father hating his own Word. God could hate the Son only if the Son were another being, that is, if polytheism or Arianism were true. But if God loved the Son, then it must be another person (besides the Son) whom God was hating during Christ's Passion. And hence that entails Nestorianism, i.e. that Christ was two persons, one divine and the other human. He loved the divine Son but hated the human Jesus. Hence the Reformed [Protestant] conception conflicts with the orthodox doctrine of the Trinity. The Father and the Son cannot be at odds. If Christ loves men, then so does the Father. Or, if the Father has wrath for men, then so does Christ. And, if the Father has wrath for the Son, then the Son must have no less wrath for Himself.[7]

---

6. For a solid explanation of the differences between the Catholic and Protestant conceptions of Christ's atonement, see this article: http://www.calledtocommunion.com/2010/04/catholic-and-reformed-conceptions-of-the-atonement/.
7. http://www.calledtocommunion.com/2010/04/catholic-and-reformed-conceptions-of-the-atonement/.

In Catholic theology, Christ made an offering of himself in love so pleasing to the Father that it super-abundantly atoned for our sins.

Before going further, realize that your goal in this discussion is not to convince your friend of the Catholic view of justification. It is instead to demonstrate to him that the Catholic view is plausible by showing that the Church's interpretation of the crucial Scripture passages is reasonable. The broader point you will make is that the Bible, taken by itself, can support varying interpretations on this topic.

ST. PAUL ON JUSTIFICATION IN THE BIBLE

Any discussion of justification will inevitably lead to Paul's Letter to the Romans, so you need to be ready to discuss the first chapters of this letter and explain how the Catholic doctrine of justification fits the text. We will examine the critical passages here; then we will see how to introduce the book of James into the dialogue.

The overall thrust of Paul's letter to the Church in Rome concerns how Gentiles—in addition to Jews—are included in God's plan of salvation through Christ. Paul explains how God kept his covenant with Israel and fulfilled his promises in Jesus Christ, offering the free gift of salvation to all.

Paul introduces his thesis early on: "For I am not ashamed of the gospel; it is the power of God for salvation to everyone who has faith, to the Jew first and also to the Greek. For in it the righteousness of God is revealed through faith for faith; as it is written, 'The one who is righteous will live by faith.'" (Rom. 1:16-17). Your Protestant friend reads these verses and thinks it should be obvious that they support *sola fide*. Why? Because he habitually reads part of verse 17 to say "the righteousness of God is revealed by faith *alone*." But the word "alone" is not there, so introducing it, even mentally, is incorrect. Catholics can affirm this verse without issue, for we also believe that justification comes through faith, but that faith is informed by *agape* (love), and that love is manifested in concrete works, which means it is not alone. You may need to explain this to your friend if he brings up this verse.

Chapter two of Romans provides the next interesting passage, one that you will probably need to bring up proactively. Paul writes, "By your stubbornness and impenitent heart, you are storing up wrath for yourself for the day of wrath and revelation of the just judgment of God, who will repay everyone according to his works: eternal life to those who seek glory, honor, and immortality through perseverance in good works" (2:5-7). Because your Protestant friend believes in justification by faith alone, he must interpret the works that Paul is speaking of here as not influencing justification in any way. In Protestant theology, the explanation of this passage goes something like this: "These works are ones that occur *after* a person is justified. So they speak to the reward that the justified will receive from God one day, but they do not in any way contribute to his justification, which is by faith alone." (A Protestant might also say that these works are part of the process of sanctification.) Further, since all those who are once-justified will remain justified—they cannot fall away—the "perseverance in good works" spoken of is really a given. By Protestant definition, all justified persons will persevere and do good works as the *fruit* of God's justifying action in them.

Recall that the Catholic Church teaches that initial justification is by grace through faith, which no works contribute to or merit in any way. So you can agree with your friend's interpretation that these works are not contributing to a Christian's *initial* justification. But it is reasonable to interpret the works mentioned as being important to one's salvation—

the eternal life spoken of by Paul. That meshes well with the Catholic belief that justification also has an *ongoing* component. Further, since under Catholic soteriology (theology of salvation) a Christian *can* abandon his faith, Paul's demand for "perseverance" isn't just a redundancy. It means that a Christian must persevere, by God's grace, or else fall away from Christ. The main idea to drive home is that this passage supports the teaching that (some kind of) works are involved in one's eternal life.

The next passages in this chapter of Romans are also an opportunity to enlighten your friend:

> For it is not the hearers of the law who are righteous in God's sight, but the doers of the law who will be justified. When Gentiles, who do not possess the law, do instinctively what the law requires, these, though not having the law, are a law to themselves. They show that what the law requires is written on their hearts, to which their own conscience also bears witness; and their conflicting thoughts will accuse or perhaps excuse them (Rom. 2:13–15).

Recall that Paul's theme in this letter concerns the inclusion of the Gentiles in God's plan of salvation through Christ. Here Paul points out that, though the Gentiles did not have the law given to the Israelites, nonetheless God wrote the *natural law* "in their hearts," and a Gentile who follows the natural law is better than an Israelite who follows the outward prescriptions of the Mosaic Law while ignoring their inner intent. For the purposes of your conversation, the takeaway here is that, although justification is indeed through faith, our actions are indispensable to a truly faithful life.

Now we come to chapter three, perhaps the most pivotal: for here your Protestant friend will be ready to quote verses as prooftexts for justification through faith alone. As you read the chapter, keep in mind that Paul is saying that following the Mosaic Law will not justify you. For the Father has sent Jesus, who justifies all people, whether Jews or Gentiles, through faith and not through works of the law. Paul summarizes his thought in verse 28: "For we hold that a person is justified by faith apart from works prescribed by the law" (Rom. 3:28). This verse aligns perfectly with Catholic doctrine. First, because the Church teaches that we are justified by faith, as the verse states. Notice the verse does not say "faith alone," but rather "faith." So this verse is not actually specific enough to provide evidence for Protestantism's doctrine of *sola fide*. Second, Catholics agree that justification does not come through the Mosaic Law, so there is no dispute there.

It is also worth pointing out that Martin Luther, in his German translation of this passage, added the word "alone" after "faith," even though (as he admitted) the original Greek verse does not include it.

Your friend here may demand that you show that faith needs to be made alive by love. To demonstrate this truth, turn to Paul's letter to the Galatians and read this verse to him: "For in Christ Jesus neither circumcision nor uncircumcision counts for anything; the only thing that counts is faith working through love" (Gal. 5:6). Note that the latter part of the verse could also be rendered "faith informed by love," where the love spoken of is *agape*, God's love. Paul does not always qualify the word *faith* this way because he assumes that the churches he is writing to, being led by the apostles and their successors, will understand what he is talking about without having to repeat everything each time he writes. There's much more in Romans 3, but if you keep in mind the aforementioned guiding principles, you will be fine.

Paul continues his arguments in the next chapter, which

tells us that Abraham's righteousness came through faith and
not through works of the law (since Abraham lived before the
Mosaic Law was instituted). Paul explains, "For the promise
that he would inherit the world did not come to Abraham
or to his descendants through the law but through the righteousness of faith" (Rom. 4:13). Here again you can agree
that righteousness (justification) comes through faith, but not
faith alone. This verse also omits the word "alone," and indeed
no verse in the entire Bible ever says we are justified through
faith alone. Point this out to your friend, and then use it as an
opportunity to bring in the book of James, which is directly
relevant as it speaks of Abraham and justification.

ST. JAMES WEIGHS IN

The book of James presents quite a pickle to Protestantism,
and though many Protestants have proposed possible interpretations of its teachings on justification, none of them are
compelling. Turn to James 2 and read the passage together
with your friend:

> Do you want to be shown, you senseless person, that faith
> apart from works is barren? Was not our ancestor Abraham
> justified by works when he offered his son Isaac on the al-
> tar? You see that faith was active along with his works, and
> faith was brought to completion by the works. Thus the
> scripture was fulfilled that says, "Abraham believed God,
> and it was reckoned to him as righteousness," and he was
> called the friend of God. You see that a person is justified
> by works and not by faith alone (James 2:20-24).

There seems here to be a contradiction between this teaching and Paul's statements that Abraham was justified by faith
and not by works. But Catholic doctrine harmonizes these

verses wonderfully. Recall that in Catholicism justification is both an initial event and a process whereby one grows in righteousness by works done through faith. So when James speaks of justification here, he is not talking of one's initial justification—to which works contribute nothing, as Catholics and Protestants both agree—but instead of one's ongoing justification. James's words also confirm Paul's in Galatians that faith working in love is true, justifying faith. Faith without love is dead.

Since Protestants believe that justification is only a one-time event, they cannot make sense of this verse. For James uses the same word for justification that Paul does, yet he clearly teaches that works are a crucial component to justification, an idea that is anathema to Protestant theology. Your friend may attempt to reconcile these verses with *sola fide* by claiming that James is talking about the works that come after justification, as the fruit of that event. Stand your ground, however, and point out that that is not what James actually says. He says a person "is justified by works and not by faith alone," so the Protestant interpretation unacceptably alters the meaning of the verses. The other option is for him to claim that in the James the same word, *justify*, is being used in a different way. Although that is possible, the apostle makes no indication that the word is being used in a special or unusual way. But even if we temporarily assumed that the usages differ, it only provides further evidence that Scripture is not so obviously clear—even on an essential issue like justification—as Protestantism's *sola scriptura* requires it to be.

CASTILE SEARCHES FOR FAITH ALONE

One day at work I sat down with a colleague for lunch. Castile was Hispanic and had grown up Catholic, but only nominally. When he went to college, he abandoned the Faith altogether and began living a hedonistic secular life.

But during an internship he was placed with two Evangelical Protestant roommates who kept encouraging him to go to their church. He didn't want to, but eventually they pestered him enough that he did it just to get them off his back. He went, and something happened: he was moved by the music, and by the people singing, and he decided to go back again the next Sunday. Soon, he was having a conversion of heart to Christ, and his life turned around.

As we had lunch together, he was naturally skeptical of Catholicism. He had grown up in it yet never came to know Jesus through it. I pointed out that it sounded as if his Catholic upbringing was weak, and he conceded that it was. Before long our conversation turned to salvation, and he asked how Catholics could get around the clear Bible passages saying we are justified through faith alone.

I had an idea here, and it played out this way.

"Castile, please find me a verse that says we are justified by faith alone." I sat back and waited.

"Oh sure it's easy." He pulled out his smart phone, went to his Bible app, did a search for faith in the New Testament and began reciting verses to me, many of the same verses we have already discussed in this chapter. He also quoted a Protestant favorite, Ephesians 2:8-9: "For by grace you have been saved through faith, and this is not your own doing; it is the gift of God—not the result of works, so that no one may boast."

It took him about four minutes to find all the verses that in his mind proved his case. Once he finished, he looked up at me, wondering how I could possibly respond to all this evidence for justification through faith alone.

I leaned in and asked, "I don't think I heard the phrase 'faith alone' in any of those passages. Is there one that says we are justified through faith 'alone'?"

He got a confused look on his face and went back to the verses, starting with Romans 3:28: "For we hold that a person is justified by faith apart from works prescribed by the law." But I pointed out that that verse did not include the word "alone" in it.

So he jumped to Ephesians 2:8-9 again, and I pointed out the same thing. The word "alone" is not there.

He went through several other verses but quit reading them aloud. Now he was looking for the word *alone* somewhere, anywhere, but he failed to find it. I said to him, "The only place you will find 'faith alone' is in James 2, where it says we are *not* justified by faith alone."

Did Castile convert back to Catholicism right there on the spot? No. It doesn't work that way. He'd had a conversion experience in an Evangelical Protestant church, and he wasn't going to leave that church, much less Protestantism, easily. But the seeds were planted: I showed him that other interpretations exist for these "prooftext" verses that he thought were slam-dunks for Protestantism.

Do not be disappointed when your friend is not convinced by your Catholic interpretation of all these verses. Justification by faith alone has been drilled into them from childhood, and in their minds departing from it or admitting any alternative interpretation of the relevant verses is tantamount to abandoning the gospel of Jesus Christ. It is enough to plant a seed. The fact is that the Catholic paradigm for justification fits the verses better than that of Protestantism.

From here you could press forward and invite your friend to study what the early Christians wrote about justification, much like you did with baptism earlier. Or perhaps this talk about justification will lead your friend to claim that, however one is justified, the Church's teaching that we can "lose our salvation" is unbiblical and false. We'll treat that subject in a bit. For now, it might be best to take these disagreements over what Scripture says about salvation as an opportunity to return to the question of whether or not the Bible is perspicuous.

YOUR PRAYER TOGETHER
"Lord, guide us to know your truth on how Christ justifies us, so that we may not be led astray into error on this important doctrine."

RECOMMENDED READING
• Romans chapters 1–3; James chapter 2
• *The Drama of Salvation,* by Jimmy Akin

6

"LET'S READ THE BIBLE TOGETHER"

MORE OFTEN THAN not, you have to be the one to initiate conversations about the faith with your friends and family. Look for a natural way to do so; for example, when discussing other topics related to God, faith, or morality. Pray and discern who God is leading you to talk to and when the right time presents itself.

But sometimes an opening can come to you.

Steven is an Evangelical Protestant friend of mine and a fellow software developer. He has an amazing mind and can solve ten problems in the time it takes me to solve one (but please don't point this out to our boss!). I had been waiting for the right time to bring up the differences between our beliefs, but never saw the opening. Then one day, after we had played soccer together, he asked why I was always so joyful, especially since I was Catholic! In his mind, Catholics believed in so many falsehoods and empty rituals that it was impossible for them to have the joy of Christ. You can't fake joy, and after years of friendship Steven saw it in me.

So began a conversation that lasted for many months. I presented the arguments on the canon and *sola scriptura* to Steven, and I could tell they made him uneasy. Our talks rarely stayed focused on any one issue, however; instead they ranged far afield into topics like morality and politics. I did my best to bring us back on track, but at the same time I tried to give reasonable Catholic answers to all his questions.

INTO UNFAMILIAR WATERS

Eventually, after I pressed him again on the canon, Steven had had enough. He was tired of defending his ship in unfamiliar waters, and he wanted to move the discussion to the Bible itself. Knowing that we disagreed on the purpose of baptism and who could be baptized, he proposed we both read all the biblical passages that mention baptism and discuss our interpretation of them. In this way, he hoped, we could come to agreement on what the Bible "clearly" said.

You can expect something like this to happen in your discussions as well. Sooner or later your friend will want to leave aside the foundational question of how we can know the content of divine revelation and instead move to the content of the Bible itself, where he will try to convince you that his interpretation of it is the correct one. This is okay. Move forward with your discussion, letting

WHERE'S THE LOVE?

Though we are focusing on intellectual arguments, remember that a powerful witness to your Protestant friend comes from your *heart*.

Pray before each meeting with your friend. Try to listen more than you speak, and really hear what he is saying. Seek to understand before seeking to be understood. And then listen for the Spirit to prompt you to share your faith.

Share your experiences in prayer, at Mass, in reading the Bible. Tell your friend, if you feel led to, about how your faith in Christ has deepened through praying the rosary. Many Protestants are highly sensitive to the emotional aspects of peoples' faith, seeing in it evidence of spiritual rebirth, a fruit of the new life that Jesus brings.

Likewise, when your friend shares with you how God has moved in his life, be ready and willing to praise God with him for his goodness. We as Catholics believe that the Holy Spirit is alive and working within our Protestant brethren and within their ecclesial communities.

him assume that *sola scriptura* is true and that the Bible comprises sixty-six books.

As your discussion continues, you can periodically remind him that these issues have not yet been resolved, but don't refuse to engage him where he feels comfortable. Any fruitful dialogue involves a give-and-take exchange where first one person gets to direct the conversation and then the other does. And even in the best case it will take your friend many months of prayer and study to come to accept the Catholic Church's claims, so covering as many of the issues that he finds important as you can will be valuable.

Now, your friend might suggest another topic to play "dueling Bible verses" with, but if you can, propose that you use baptism as the topic. Usually your friend will accept this because he's confident that his reading of the Bible on *any* topic will be easily shown to be true, but also because he will think that the biblical verses on baptism, especially, are a slam-dunk in his favor. You will show him otherwise! (If, however, some other topic is chosen, do not fear. You can use a good Catholic study Bible, the *Catechism*, and Catholic books that specifically tackle that other topic, to prepare.

SAILING INTO THE BAPTISMAL WATERS

You can find all the verses that explicitly mention baptism by using a concordance. Do an online search for "bible concordance" and you will find some handy online tools. (Many Bibles also include a partial concordance as an appendix.) Be sure to look up not only "baptism" but also variants like "baptized." Read the notes in a Catholic study Bible (for example, the Ignatius Study Bible) to get an idea of how the Church interprets them. These verses are your starting point for discussion.

Also, read the *Catechism* on baptism and don't miss the

biblical references that support the Church's teachings. For instance, 1215 states, "This sacrament is also called '*the washing of regeneration and renewal by the Holy Spirit*,' for it signifies and actually brings about the birth of water and the Spirit without which no one 'can enter the kingdom of God.'" Then the *Catechism* references Titus 3:5 and John 3:5, neither of which probably showed up in the concordance search for "baptism." This is because both those verses are talking about baptism but don't mention the word itself. Yet they are crucial to understanding—and explaining to your friend—the true teaching on baptism. (We're still missing one other important source for supporting the Church's teachings on baptism— the writings of the early Christians—but we will leave that for a later chapter.)

You must understand that Protestant beliefs on baptism are as diverse as the number of denominations. Some churches baptize infants, others don't; some do full immersion only, some allow pouring or sprinkling; some believe that baptism is ordinarily necessary for salvation, some don't; some believe that baptism is purely symbolic, others think it is more. You need to ask your friend what he believes about baptism and why. His answer will invariably include the listing of biblical verses that he interprets in support of his belief. That's a good starting point, when it's your turn to respond, for talking about the Catholic beliefs on baptism.

Although Protestant teachings on baptism are diverse, most believe that baptism, while important, is mainly a symbolic gesture, one that shows the church community that you have given your life to Christ. Catholics, on the other hand, believe in baptismal *regeneration*. When we are baptized, the Holy Spirit comes to dwell within us. We are remade, becoming a new creation in Christ (see 2 Cor. 5:17 and Gal. 6:15). The original sin we inherited from Adam is washed away, as well as any actual sins we have committed in our life (if we are over the age of reason; babies have not committed any actual sins). We are made God's children and enter a state of sanctifying grace, where God's divine life resides within us. Few, if any, Protestants believe in baptismal regeneration to this extent, which is one reason why baptism is a good discussion topic to use when getting to this stage in your conversation.

After learning what your friend believes about baptism, present the Catholic teaching and explain how you interpret the verses to support it. Start with John 3:3-5: "Jesus answered him, 'Very truly, I tell you, no one can see the kingdom of God without being born from above.' Nicodemus said to him, 'How can anyone be born after having grown old? Can one enter a second time into the mother's womb and be born?' Jesus answered, 'Very truly, I tell you, no one can enter the kingdom of God without being born of water and Spirit.'"

Protestants love these verses, as they are the source of the doctrine that one must be "born again" to be saved. The Greek text of verse three can be translated "born again" or "born anew" or "born from above." Notice that Nicodemus completely misses the meaning of Christ's words, taking them in a purely natural sense. He is thinking of a person's physical birth from his mother. So Jesus reiterates the same teaching— that one must be born again—in a different way, saying that anyone who wants to enter the kingdom of God must be "born of water and the Spirit."

I asked a Protestant friend what he thought Jesus meant by "water and the Spirit," and he said that the water meant natural childbirth, whereas the Spirit meant supernatural birth via a conversion experience. Is that plausible? Not really, because Jesus uses the combination "water *and* the Spirit" in his second statement as a direct correlation to being "born anew." Somehow water and the Spirit will be combined such that a person is born from above by God. The answer is right in front of us: to be "born anew" one must be baptized in water, and in doing so one receives the Spirit.

These verses don't mention baptism explicitly, but the connections to baptism elsewhere in the New Testament and early Church are evident. Ask your friend how he interprets these verses. There really is no good answer other than the Catholic one, and it can be troubling for a Protestant to imagine that the source verses for the hallmark phrase "being born again" support the Catholic interpretation, so be prepared for any kind of response. After discussing this passage in John 3, ask your friend what he makes of 1 Peter 3:21: "And baptism, which this prefigured, now saves you—not as a removal of dirt from the body, but as an appeal to God for a good conscience, through the resurrection of Jesus Christ." Make sure you have read your Catholic study Bible's notes on these verses before bringing them up. These verses directly connect baptism with salvation, which causes Protestant theologians to twist themselves into pretzels to come up with alternative interpretations.

He will likely respond by bringing up verses that he feels support the symbolic interpretation of baptism. He will provide alternative interpretations of the verses you mention. Realize that, under Protestantism's principle of *sola scriptura*, there is no way to resolve your differing interpretations, because each person has just as much authority to interpret the Bible as anyone else. Nonetheless, do your best to engage him on the interpretation he provides.

An important thing to keep in mind at this point in your discussion (and throughout your conversations) is that you should be willing to concede points when you can. If an interpretation is offered that you consider plausible, say so. "I can see how that verse could be interpreted that way, and although I don't think that's the correct interpretation, given your other beliefs it makes sense for you to read it that way." Being willing to concede some things demonstrates that you are reasonable and not trying to just win an argument. Of course, you cannot concede a point that is false and that you can refute, but not every point is this critical.

THE GOAL OF ARGUING OVER VERSE INTERPRETATIONS

Although it *can* be profitable to go into great depth in exploring verses—an entire biblical science is devoted to this very study—in my experience it is best to avoid spending too much time trying to argue over a set of verses. You want to get to the root of the differences that are causing your conflicting interpretations, and that root is *authority*. Your friend has accepted someone else's interpretation (and framework for interpretation) as authoritative, even if he doesn't realize it. And you have, too, by accepting the authority of the Catholic Church. The difference is that you know you have accepted one while he may not know that he has. One of the main goals of your dialogue will be to help him see that he has indeed ascribed to an authority. Then the question becomes, "Is that authority credible?" My friend Steven and I finally hit the wall of conflicting interpretations on baptism. Interestingly, at that point he wanted to give up on our entire discussion, arguing that he was just looking at the "plain words of Scripture," whereas I was being told by the Catholic Church what to think. He was really bothered by the fact that the Catholic Church claims to be infallible under certain conditions. To him, this claim was both arrogant and made dialogue worthless, since I "took orders" from the Church and therefore would never be open to considering an alternative interpretation of the Bible.

His objection is understandable. Why argue with someone

who thinks he is following an infallible entity? Such a person will never think he can be wrong, and so will never be open to changing his mind. Speaking from my own experience, I was once a militant atheist and would have told you that I was certain that my ideas were right. Then I became an Evangelical Protestant. As an Evangelical Protestant, I was likewise certain my beliefs were true and that the Catholic Church was false. Then I became a Catholic. We all think our beliefs are true and most people hold firmly to that conviction, but as is seen from my conversion and the conversions of countless others, that does not mean that one cannot or will not ever be persuaded that they are wrong, in big or in small ways.

Another consequence to the inevitable impasse over how to interpret Scripture on baptism or any other subject is that it leads to the topic of whether Scripture is able to be readily understood on its own. For your friend, the meaning of biblical verses seems quite clear. He has likely been taught that anyone can pick up the Bible, read it with sincere faith, and come to a true understanding of God and Christianity. Sure, some verses are hard to understand or may at first be confusing, but another verse or set of verses will unlock that difficult part and make it comprehensible. ("Scripture interprets Scripture" is their maxim here.)

This idea that the Bible's meaning is clear is called the "perspicuity" of Scripture. Since your friend likely believes in it, it will seem to him that your different interpretation of the verses on baptism must mean that *you* are not able to understand the clear meaning of the Bible. And so you will need to challenge him on the idea of perspicuity.

YOUR PRAYER TOGETHER

"Father, we believe that you inspired Scripture and commanded us to be baptized. May our conversation not cause us to doubt our faith in you, but spur us on to seek to understand Scripture in its fullness."

RECOMMENDED READING
• The *Catechism* on baptism: 1213–1284
• John 3:1–21
• Ignatius Study Bible (New Testament)

PART II

MAKING HEADWAY

7

CHALLENGING PERSPICUITY

PROTESTANTS BELIEVE THAT the Bible is clear enough that any literate and faithful person can understand it, at least on those topics deemed "essential." This doctrine of the *perspicuity of Scripture* was championed by Martin Luther, the most famous Protestant Reformer. If one passage is unclear, perspicuity says, another one will illuminate it. This belief is a necessary support to *sola scriptura*, for if the Bible alone is the sole infallible rule of faith, then it very well needs to be comprehensible by everyone who reads it.

Some Protestants will qualify this doctrine by explaining that average Christians—those not able to understand Hebrew and Greek, for example—should take advantage of the scholarship and research of Christians more learned than themselves. In this way, though parts of the Bible may confuse them, they can look to these wise scholars and come to a correct understanding. Pastors, Sunday school leaders, theology professors, and the authors of the notes in various study Bibles are good sources of this wisdom. The idea here is that the Bible is clear but does sometimes require an expert on language, theology, and history for full understanding.

CLEARLY DEBATABLE

To challenge this doctrine, first remind your friend of the existence of many different Protestant denominations, each professing to follow the clear teaching of Scripture but nonetheless contradicting one another in numerous areas. Whether you count dozens of such groups or thousands, it is strong circumstantial evidence against perspicuity. Your friend may try to claim in reply that such conflicts are only on non-essential issues. "We agree on all the essentials, and that's all that matters," is a popular refrain. This response can be used as a springboard to talk about the core question of authority. Who gets to decide which issues are essential and which are not? Where in the Bible does it categorize different teachings in this way? And if the Bible doesn't do that, where does it spell out the process by which a Christian can figure out how to categorize them?

> ### THE CONVERSATION GETS TENSE
>
> Sooner or later one of your discussions will become heated. One of you will interrupt the other or will feel like you are not being understood, or that your position is not being fairly portrayed, and soon tempers are flaring.
>
> Don't be too alarmed by it. In a sense it is a good thing to get heated, since it means both of you are passionate in your beliefs and zealous for the truth. If necessary, take a break for a while and feed your friendship by discussing other topics.

Your friend will most likely respond that issues like salvation and Christ's divinity are highly important issues and therefore obviously essential. You can then ask him why, then, if most Protestant denominations agree on those issues, they have split from one another so many times. He may argue that most of those splits were due to personality conflicts, the sin of pride, and other non-doctrinal reasons. But this is not the case historically. Most splits in Protestant churches occurred when one person or group of people concluded that the church was teaching falsely on an essential issue. For example, in the early 1900s the non-populous Pentecostal movement within Protestantism fractured over the doctrine of the Trinity, with the so-called "Oneness Pentecostals" denying the Church's traditional dogma of the Trinity, and instead teaching a form of the Modalist heresy where the Father, Son, and Holy Spirit are not divine Persons, but rather merely three different manifestations or modes of God.

Closer to my home, one of the local Evangelical Protestant churches that my friends went to split because the associate pastor interpreted Revelation differently than did the head pastor. He broke off and took a large chunk of the church with him. The history of Protestantism is replete with such divisions over doctrinal issues.

Splits can also occur when one party considers an issue to be essential but the other doesn't. Recently I read a story about a young-earth creationist—someone who believes that the earth is only several thousand years old and that the creation story in Genesis must be taken strictly literally—who condemned a fellow Protestant for proposing that the "days" in Genesis could be taken figuratively, especially given the scientific consensus that the earth is billions of years old. The young-earth creationist declared the other man to be in heresy, while the other explained that he didn't think this issue was serious enough to become divided over. It only takes one side to decide that an issue is essential!

Another reply you may hear is that some Christians fail to interpret Scripture correctly because they aren't listening to the Holy Spirit well enough, perhaps because they are too influenced by the world or by sinful desires. In any given case this might be true, of course, but there is no way in Protestantism to resolve this finger-pointing, as each side claims to be the one listening to the Spirit. The other side is always at fault.

You might respond by saying that you have known faithful Christians with sincere beliefs on both sides of contentious issues, each as sincere, intelligent, and holy as the other. So it seems improbable that differences in interpretation can be attributed simply to some groups' lack of faith or prayer. A more likely explanation is that the Bible is not as clear as Protestants need it to be to make *sola scriptura* work.

THE CHURCH MAKES THE BIBLE CLEAR

The Catholic Church teaches that Christians should read the Bible regularly. But the Bible should be read in its proper home—the Church—under the illumination of the apostolic Tradition and the guidance of the teaching authority of the Church. The apostles handed on the truth of divine revelation to their successors, and the Holy Spirit preserved this truth in the Church, so it makes sense—especially since Scripture's meaning is not always clear—to read the Bible in light of this revealed Tradition, of which it is a part. Furthermore, the Church enjoins us to read Scripture as a whole, keeping in mind the content and unity of the entire Bible rather than taking books or passages piecemeal. God is the primary author of Scripture, and the books fit together and mutually illuminate one another. But these connections are not always obvious. It requires the divine guidance given to the Church.

For instance, if we looked at the Lord's Supper in Matthew 26 and asked how Jesus is present in Holy Communion, what other Bible passages should we select to clarify this verse? If we pointed to the verses where Jesus speaks figuratively of being the vine or the gate, we might conclude that he must have been speaking only symbolically when he said, "This is my body." But if we take the end of John 6, where Jesus speaks in visceral language of the need to eat his flesh and drink his blood, we could conclude that he must have been speaking of a substantial, metaphysical change in the consecration of the Eucharist. It is not clear to the individual twenty-first-century Bible reader which passages are the correct ones to use, and in truth both of them have plausible-sounding reasons that argue for their inclusion.

In the section of the *Catechism* on the Eucharist, we are given the way to interpret the Last Supper accurately:

> At the heart of the eucharistic celebration are the bread and wine that, by the words of Christ and the invocation of the Holy Spirit, become Christ's Body and Blood. Faithful to the Lord's command the Church continues to do, in his memory and until his glorious return, what he did on the eve of his Passion: "He took bread. . . . " "He took the cup filled with wine. . . . " The signs of bread and wine become, in a way surpassing understanding, the Body and Blood of Christ (CCC 1333).

On this doctrine and on others, the Church makes clear what the Lord has revealed to it through Scripture and Tradition. We think with the Church by seeking to understand what it teaches and why. And we are rewarded by being able to read Scripture without fear of going off the rails and interpreting it wrongly.

DEGREES OF CLARITY

Another tack that your friend might take is to point out that many passages in the Bible *are* quite clear. Your arguments against perspicuity have likely made him feel that you are saying the Bible isn't clear at all, but isn't it clear, for example, in Genesis that God created the universe? Or in the Gospel of John that God loved the world and sent his Son to save it? And here you can concede his point. Many of the meanings contained in the Bible are clear enough that most anyone (without an agenda) could understand them. And so many people have come to believe in Christ just by reading the Bible and praying. They are truly God's words and, by the power of the Holy Spirit, can and do pierce hearts and change lives. Catholics believe all this, too, and in this we can agree with Protestants.

But if these undeniably clear parts were the only essentials, then we would not have the divisions within Protestantism that continue to this day. For as we saw, division tends not to occur over non-essentials. We still need an explanation why Christians disagree over things in Scripture that are unclear *and* essential—and the Bible's lack of perspicuity is the key suspect. The waters of the ocean may be clear on the surface and a few feet below it, but as you dive into the depths they get murky, and you need a light to see. The infallible Magisterium of the Church uses the light of Tradition to illuminate the depths of Scripture.

ENDING THE STANDOFF

But the impasse over how to interpret the Bible on baptism still remains. In fact, it is just magnified by your disagreement over perspicuity. How can progress be made?

Recall that you brought up in this discussion how apostles transmitted to their successors the deposit of faith given to them by God. That was a bold claim, and your friend will be curious about it. "Tradition" has a bad connotation to most Protestants. Jesus often condemned human traditions in the Bible, decrying that they were used to supplant divine truth. So your claim of an apostolic Tradition that isn't explicitly written down in Scripture will seem highly suspect to your friend.

This tension provides the perfect opportunity to bring in

your "ace in the hole": the Church Fathers and their writings. Not only will they support this idea of succession from the apostles and the Tradition they received from them, but they will also shine light on baptism, providing a powerful argument for the Catholic position and bringing your discussion even closer to the central question of authority.

Before we reveal our ace though, we need to spend the next chapter digging a bit into the mind of your Protestant friend, and what he may be going through as you present all this evidence to him.

YOUR PRAYER TOGETHER

"Dear Jesus, we disagree over the clarity of the Bible and seek your wisdom in knowing how you meant your inspired words to be understood. Give us keen discernment in this matter so that we can reach the unity that you prayed we would have."

RECOMMENDED READING

• The *Catechism* on the Eucharist: 1322–1419
• John 6:52–71
• *The Catholic Controversy,* by St. Francis de Sales

8

FIGHTING
SEASICKNESS

BY THIS POINT, you have presented information and arguments that your friend never knew about. And he probably feels queasy, like a landlubber heading out to sea for the first time. Though he may appear confident on the outside, from my experience a Protestant cannot remain unfazed after being exposed to a barrage of data that runs counter to what he believes.

When we reached this point in our dialogue, my Evangelical friend Steven told me, "I feel like I'm in a house built on big wooden stilts, and you're standing at the bottom shaking and rattling them! It's wobbling around, and I don't know what to make of it."

Don't expect your friend to be this candid, but know that this is quite possibly what he is going through.

YOUR FRIEND'S DILEMMA
Let's delve into his head a bit. He believes Jesus is real. He knows that Jesus loves him. He has seen him work in his life. Further, he knows that the Bible must contain divine truth because reading it and putting its words into practice have changed him. *And he is right!* The Bible *does* contain the truth of divine revelation, and Jesus is real and does love him. And Jesus *has* worked in his life and continues to do so.

The conundrum that he faces, then, is how to reconcile this with the strong evidence you're presenting for the Catholic Church. His perception and understanding of Jesus has been formed through the lens of Protestantism, and specifically whatever flavor of Protestant church he goes to. His beliefs on theological and moral issues likewise differ in big and in small ways from Catholicism's. He is not willing to abandon his faith in Jesus or in the Bible.

Here is where you have to reassure him that in becoming Catholic he would not have to. Instead, he would be embracing the fullness of the truths that he *already believes in.* He would keep believing in Jesus *and* also get to receive him in the Eucharist. His trust in the Holy Spirit and his divine aid would not be diminished, but would flourish to its full extent when he received the sacrament of confirmation. As a Protestant, he (sometimes waveringly) hopes that he is forgiven when he privately confesses his sins in his heart to God, but if he became a Catholic, he would have the confident assurance of forgiveness in the words of absolution spoken to him by Christ's priest in the sacrament of confession.

PRAYING FOR YOUR FRIEND

If you are not already doing so, remember to pray for your friend as you continue your dialogue. Nothing is more important. A single prayer made in faith is stronger than all the arguments presented here because conversion is ultimately wrought by God.

Although presenting this information is crucial, it represents only the human part that God has given us to do. The supernatural part is done by him, but he invites us to be a part of his work, too, through prayer.

And as Catholics we are not alone when we pray. Enlist the intercession of the saints, including the Church Fathers, in storming heaven for your friend. We are all united in Christ's Mystical Body, the Church, and share in the communion of saints. Continue to pray for your friend whenever he comes to your mind. It may take a long time, but God will never stop inviting him into the fullness of the truth in the Catholic Church.

As simple and appealing as this sounds to Catholics, none of it will be easy for your friend to accept right away. His faith in Jesus is tangled with a particular set of beliefs on a host of issues. Separating the one from the others is incredibly difficult. He has to be able to see that, even though some of his beliefs are inaccurate or incomplete, they don't mean his belief in Jesus is in error. No, his belief in Jesus is true and beautiful, but his understanding of Jesus and of Christian truth has come through human intermediaries—and that introduces the possibility of error.

And so he must ask himself, "Who are those intermediaries and why do I trust them?" Following this line of thought begins with his current Protestant church, moves outward to his church's parent denomination (or nondenomination), then back through history to the denomination's beginning, and ultimately to the Protestant Reformation and the original Reformers (Luther, Calvin, Zwingli, the Anabaptists, the Anglicans, etc.).

But it's not yet time to go that far in your discussion. It is enough now to reassure him that the Catholic Church believes him to be a Christian, that he has the Holy Spirit dwelling within him, and that many of his beliefs are indeed solid. The Catholic Church is the perfection of his Protestant faith, not the abolishment of it. In becoming Catholic, he is not leaving the waters of divine truth, but rather swimming from the shallow pools into the deep ocean. He is not abandoning Scripture, but embracing it in its fullness and learning its true meaning.

More than any other time, this is when you must show yourself to be his good friend, one who is patient and respectful of him and his beliefs. Having one's foundations shaken is unsettling, and the messenger who causes this can be an object of suspicion. Some of your conversations may have even gotten tense at times, in spite of your best efforts, and those occasions can increase this suspicion that maybe you don't have what's best for him at heart. All you can do is show humility and genuine interest in him and be discerning in how you proceed.

For years I had such discussions with a friend of mine, Brant, and eventually we hit a time where I couldn't really influence him anymore. He had been coming around to the Catholic way of seeing things, and he started to fear he was going to be cut loose from his Christian moorings altogether. This thought frightened him, though I didn't perceive it at the time. Only when he cooled off toward me and started avoiding our lunchtime chats did I realize he needed some space. He needed to talk to other people, to go online and converse with other Catholics on blogs and through email. He had been rattled, it is true, but he was not completely certain that I was presenting him with the full story of Catholicism and Protestantism, so he needed outside confirmation. Sometimes I would encounter his comments on an apologetics blog I frequented; he was asking them questions and probing with arguments. The Catholics who responded to him did so with aplomb, reassuring him that he was on the right track, and offering their unique perspectives to him on what it was like to become Catholic.

So Brant discovered that I was not misleading him, and a year or so later he surprised me by telling me that he was going to become Catholic. He and his family all entered full communion the following Easter. His eldest daughter was baptized, and my wife and I were chosen to be her godparents.

ANTI-CATHOLICISM BY OSMOSIS

Back to the general psychology of your Protestant friend: Another common cause of seasickness at this stage is anti-Catholic bias. Many Protestants not only have doctrinal beliefs that conflict with the Church's, but also some degree of prejudice against (as well as misconceptions about) the Church itself. Although your discussions will allow you to clear up and work through his prejudices, you can't expect instantly to correct all the deep-seated mistrust of Catholicism that many Protestants have built up since childhood.

He has likely heard his pastors talk about the Catholic Church as a man-made religion or worse. His parents or trusted Christian mentors may have explained to him that Catholics aren't Christians due to their false beliefs. He may have been told that Catholics worship Mary, try to conjure the souls of dead people, believe that their works will save them instead of Jesus, and so on. Even if intellectually his experience in talking about the Faith with you has cast doubt on these things he was told, there's still enough smoke to make him think that there also must be a fire somewhere.

ELIZABETH'S STORY OF
OVERCOMING ANTI-CATHOLIC BIASES

My friend Elizabeth grew up in a Protestant home. Her father was and is a pastor in the Assemblies of God. She was taught from an early age to reverence Scripture and the charismatic gifts of the Spirit. She was also taught that Catholicism was false and evil.

By the end of high school, she believed God was calling her to be a missionary to foreign countries. She planned to go to Bible college and then enter the mission fields, probably in the historically Catholic countries of South America. But God had other plans. She met a Protestant missionary from Mongolia who was visiting the United States; they fell in love, and a few years later were married.

He went to seminary in hopes of being a Protestant pastor. Elizabeth began blogging. She wrote an article on October

31st of one year that celebrated the birth of the Protestant Reformation. A Catholic woman commented that the Reformation was nothing to celebrate, as it wrought great devastation upon the Church, wounding the unity that Christ desired in John 17.

Elizabeth was taken aback. This was the first time she had ever encountered a Catholic who seemed to love Jesus and know her faith. Sometime later, she found a blog post written by my wife Catherine. The post talked about the feminine genius developed by Pope St. John Paul II. So much of its content resonated with Elizabeth that she started to read more on Catholicism.

She discovered eucharistic adoration and went to a chapel to try it out. To her amazement, she palpably felt Christ's real presence there. She went home shaken but did not dare tell her husband about it. Quietly, she learned more of the Catholic Faith. Her two favorite authors—Tolkien and G.K. Chesterton—she found out were Catholic. "Catholicism has gotten much right," she said to herself one day, "but why then do I believe it's wrong on so many things?"

She continued going to adoration, and one night after being with Jesus in the chapel, she had a dream. In it, a plumb line hung down from the ceiling, with the Eucharist attached to the end. She knew God was showing her that it was by the truth of the Eucharist that she must measure every other teaching. If the Eucharist were true, the Mass was true. If the Mass was true, Catholicism was true.

She told her husband about her journey, and while he couldn't join her—at least not yet—he respected her convictions. She entered RCIA, and her two eldest children made the decision to enter as well.

Elizabeth's anti-Catholic upbringing was ultimately overcome through a series of events, beginning with a single blog comment from a faithful Catholic. God led that woman to plant the seed; he fertilized it; and subsequently more people gathered the harvest.

JASON, AN UNLIKELY CONVERT

I met Jason via Twitter, of all places. He and I began corresponding, but I learned he was already heading down the path to the Catholic Church.

His conversion to Christ, however, was anything but Catholic. At 19 years of age, he accepted Christ and became a Protestant Christian. He imbibed the anti-Catholic writings of Jack Chick, but then moved on to more substantial anti-Catholicism found in the works of John MacArthur, R.C. Sproul, and John Piper.

By his early twenties he was saying things like:

"I don't know how anyone can be a Catholic and be saved." "Catholicism is the world's biggest cult." "The Gospel of Rome is not a gospel at all. Gospel means 'good news,' and sending billions of people to hell is not good news at all."

But on an airplane flight, he happened to sit next to a professor at a Catholic seminary. They conversed for an hour and a half, going back and forth about theology, and Jason emerged from it thinking it might be possible for Catholics to be in heaven after all.

Jason softened toward Catholicism, but was not close to converting. Years passed; he met his future wife and they married and had children. They decided to homeschool their children, and one day at a homeschool group party, he met Francis, the father of one of the other children. Francis was Catholic, and by inspecting Jason's bookshelf he quickly realized that he was dealing with a fervent Protestant.

Francis had studied Catholic apologetics for years and immediately engaged Jason on *sola scriptura* and justification through faith alone. Jason was surprised but always eager to argue on these topics, and they began a series of conversations that went on for months. Each recommended different reading materials to the other, and they argued about them when they met.

Francis recommended *The Protestant's Dilemma* to Jason, and he devoured it. Jason began to get seasick with what he discovered, but he still refused to convert. He decided he had to learn about what the earliest Christians had to say about the Faith, so he started reading the Church Fathers. Dumbstruck by how Catholic they were, he entered RCIA.

In spite of having gulped down to its deepest dregs so many anti-Catholic writings, Jason followed the truth wherever it led him. It took a Catholic professor, a sharp and bold Catholic dad, a Catholic Answers book, and the Church Fathers to break down the barriers between him and Christ's Church.

The Church Fathers were key to Jason's conversion. It is time to get back to our discussion on baptism and for you to use the Church Fathers as your ace in the hole. Trim the sails: sharp's the word and quick's the action!

YOUR PRAYER TOGETHER
"Heavenly Father, we are finite and weak, and are so easily confused. Dispel the darkness that so often surrounds our thoughts and show us your glorious face."

READING RECOMMENDATIONS
• John chapter 17
• Decree on Ecumenism (*Unitatis Redintegratio*) from the Second Vatican Council

9

INTRODUCING THE CHURCH FATHERS

YOUR PROTESTANT FRIEND may have never heard of the Church Fathers (I certainly hadn't when I was a Protestant). These were faithful and influential Christians teachers, pastors, and leaders who taught and defended the Faith from the late first century through the sixth. Many, though not all, are considered saints by the Catholic Church.

Given the impasse you face about how to interpret the Bible on baptism, it makes sense to bring in other evidence. And though your friend may not know much about the Fathers, he will likely be favorably disposed to hearing what the early Christians believed, since (especially with the Fathers of the first couple of centuries) there wouldn't have been much time for the teachings of Jesus and the apostles to have been corrupted. So, what did these early Christians have to say about baptism?

THE CHURCH FATHERS ON BAPTISM

Start by sharing with your friend what St. Justin Martyr wrote about baptismal regeneration in the middle of the second century:

> I will also relate the manner in which we dedicated ourselves to God when we had been made new through

Christ; lest, if we omit this, we seem to be unfair in the explanation we are making. As many as are persuaded and believe that what we teach and say is true, and undertake to be able to live accordingly, are instructed to pray and to entreat God with fasting, for the remission of their sins that are past; we praying and fasting with them.

They then are brought by us where there is water, and are regenerated in the same manner in which we were ourselves regenerated. For, in the name of God, the Father and Lord of the universe, and of our Savior Jesus Christ, and of the Holy Spirit, they then receive the washing with water.... The reason for this we have received from the apostles.[8]

And this food is called among us the Eucharist, of which no one is allowed to partake but the man who believes that the things which we teach are true, and who has been washed with the washing that is for the remission of sins, and unto regeneration, and who is so living as Christ has enjoined.[9]

Notice how Justin explains that baptismal regeneration remits our sins but also reveals that this teaching was received from the apostles. Justin was born around the time of St. John's death, so many Christians of his era still had living memories of the apostles themselves.

Another great Church Father from the second century who witnessed to the truth of baptismal regeneration was St. Irenaeus, bishop of Lyons, a disciple of St. Polycarp who himself was a disciple of St. John. Irenaeus pulls no punches in pointing out that to deny baptism's regenerating effects is to renounce the entire Christian faith.

8. St. Justin Martyr, *First Apology* Chapter 61.
9. St. Justin Martyr, *First Apology* Chapter 66.

And when we come to refute them [i.e., those heretics], we shall show in its fitting-place, that this class of men have been instigated by Satan to a denial of that baptism which is regeneration to God, and thus to a renunciation of the whole [Christian] faith.[10]

This is only a small selection. Both of these saints wrote even more about baptismal regeneration, as did other Church Fathers and early Christians in the second century.[11] Once we get to the third century, the writings that support baptismal regeneration multiply.[12] This early Christian witness to baptismal regeneration is unanimous. If this teaching were heretical and contradicted the apostles, you would expect at least a few leaders in the early Church to have stood up in protest of it, but not a single one does—or even offers an alternative interpretation for the relevant verses.

Present this historical evidence to your friend and give him time to respond. But be careful: the Church Fathers are Catholic to the core, and their writings contain many teachings that simply aren't reconcilable with Protestant doctrine. You'll want to introduce them to your friend gently and give him time to absorb the evidence they provide for the Catholic Church.

Some Protestants put little stock into what ancient Christians wrote, unless it is explicitly contained in the New Testament itself, so your friend may simply dismiss these writings.

10. St. Irenaeus, *Against Heresies* I.21.
11. See the *Epistle of Barnabas*, Chapter 11; the *Shepherd of Hermas*, ninth Similitude, Chapter 16; and St. Theophilus, bishop of Antioch's letter *To Autolycus*, Book II.
12. A good reference for Church Fathers' writings that included teaching on baptismal regeneration is Called to Communion's article on the subject: http://www.calledtocommunion.com/2010/06/the-church-fathers-on-baptismal-regeneration/.

He may propose that they're forgeries or that they represent a misleading sample of what the early Christians believed. You can patiently explain that even Protestant historians accept these works as genuine and as representative of what was being taught in the early Church. It's not totally impossible that they represent a minority view, that other early Christians were teaching doctrines in agreement with modern Protestantism, but the simple fact is there's no existing evidence that there were.

THE PROTESTANT'S DILEMMA ON THE CHURCH FATHERS

Given their authenticity, only two options remain to explain the Fathers' testimony to baptismal regeneration: either what they taught faithfully preserved and transmitted what the apostles taught, or what they taught was false, indicating that the apostles' teachings had already been corrupted after less than a century.

ROCKY SHOAL: CATHOLICS DON'T KNOW THE BIBLE

Your Protestant friend says: "For all your talk of how much the Bible is revered by the Catholic Church, I've never met a Catholic who regularly read the Bible, let alone studied it deeply."

In response, you can point out that:

- "I regularly read the Bible"— and make sure that you can say so honestly!

- Long before Protestantism existed, from the early Church on, countless Catholics became Scripture scholars

- Catholics hear more Scripture read during Mass over the year than most Protestants do in their services

- Many nominal Catholics don't know the Bible, but then many nominal Protestants don't either, which is why you have to compare apples to apples: devout Catholics with devout Protestants

If the former is true, then the Catholic Church is right on baptismal regeneration and the vast majority of Protestant churches are wrong. That's huge. And it is something that your friend will find almost impossible to concede, so don't expect it. Think of it as one more pebble placed on the Catholic side of the scale of evidence in his mind.

If the latter is true and the apostles' teachings became corrupted in the second century,[13] then all Christians are in big trouble, for we have no way of knowing what books even belong in the Bible. You see, these same early Christians from the second, third, and fourth centuries were the ones who discerned which books God had inspired and which he had not. If the Church leaders who lived just one generation after the apostles were believing and teaching a corrupted Christianity, we can have little trust that they and their successors correctly discerned the books that belong in the Bible. The Holy Spirit apparently let them fall into error. And since Protestantism bases its entire body of doctrine from the Bible alone, an untrustworthy Bible means an untrustworthy Christianity.

If your friend does elect this second option, a thought-provoking question to present to him is this: "Imagine you lived around A.D. 100. The apostles are all dead, and now their disciples are leading the Church. Given that the New Testament books were not yet codified, would you trust the teachings of these direct disciples of the apostles?"

You can then ask him why he would trust them or why

13. Protestants commonly believe that corruption entered the visible Church in the early centuries. Few are willing to nail down an exact date, but most agree that by the fifth or sixth century, false teachings, accretions, and general "Romish superstitions" crept their way into the churches, monasteries, and papist hearts. For some, a remnant of "true believers" existed in hidden places until the Protestant Reformation; for others, the true faith was rediscovered by the Reformation. Mormons call this alleged falling away the Great Apostasy and mark the date as happening soon after the death of the last apostle. However, few Protestants are willing to say that already in the A.D. 100s the apostasy had occurred. Most would set the earliest date in the 300s or later, so it is eye-opening to demonstrate that, based on their Protestant beliefs, already in the second century grave errors were widespread on important doctrines.

he wouldn't. Either way, this question can lead to a fruitful discussion. It is powerful because it places your friend in an environment where living by the Bible alone was not possible. Yet this situation was a real one that all Christians in the first centuries of the Church found themselves in. It highlights the anachronistic nature of *sola scriptura*, revealing its impossibility as the guiding doctrine of the early Church.

PROTESTANTS VERSUS TIMOTHY AND TITUS

One time I debated a Protestant apologist and this very issue came up. He claimed all books of the Bible had been written by A.D. 70, and at the instant the last one was finished, *sola scriptura* kicked in and became the lone infallible rule of faith, trumping any other source of teaching. The problem for him was that some of the apostles were still alive at that time, as were many of their authorized successors, men like Timothy and Titus. My Protestant debate partner was backed into a corner and forced to admit that, had he lived during that time, he would have taken his own interpretation of Scripture over that of the apostles themselves.

Consider that Paul wrote Timothy two letters to help him pastor the Church in Ephesus. Now imagine a Christian who lived at that time—let's call him David—listening to a sermon that Timothy gave on one of Paul's letters to him. David politely raises his hand and says to Timothy: "Um, sorry Pastor Timothy, but you are misinterpreting Paul's letter to you. It actually means this . . . " The hubris would be farcical if it were not so disturbing. Yet that is exactly what Protestants are forced to admit they believe, if they claim that *sola scriptura* became operative the moment the ink dried on the last book of the New Testament.

Coming back to our main topic, the Church Fathers are a great ally to you in your life of faith and in your dialogue with Protestants. For every one passage in their works that could possibly be construed as being Protestant-leaning, there are fifty more that are unequivocally Catholic. Your goal is to expose your friend to them in a way that will encourage him to read more of their works on his own. This can only aid him in seeing how strong the evidence is for the Catholic Church.

Even with all the evidence you have presented to support the doctrine of baptismal regeneration, it is likely that he will continue to say he's unconvinced. To him, it's still obvious that the Bible teaches symbolic-only baptism, but he probably doesn't realize that this interpretation has been greatly influenced by the Protestant Reformers. The next step in your dialogue will be to unveil the Reformers and demonstrate his unintentional reliance on them for his beliefs.

YOUR PRAYER TOGETHER

"Father, we wish to know the apostolic Faith that Jesus taught his disciples and they taught the early Christians. Shine your light upon our hearts so that we can discover where this Faith may be found. We ask this in Jesus' name, Amen."

RECOMMENDED READING

• The Epistle of St. Ignatius of Antioch to the Ephesians
• *Handed Down*, by James L. Papandrea

10

RECOGNIZING THE INFLUENCE OF THE REFORMERS

IN THIS CONVERSATION, your task is to help your friend realize that his particular Christian beliefs have been significantly influenced by other human beings, especially the men known as the Protestant Reformers. No matter which Protestant denomination he belongs to, the Reformers' ideas have shaped his framework for interpreting the Bible, even though he probably doesn't realize this (yet).

Recall that you and he still have not reached a resolution about baptism's purpose. You offered a reasonable alternative interpretation of the pertinent biblical passages. You then submitted some of the Church Fathers' testimony. And though he may remain unconvinced, he has discovered that the case is not as simple as he had always thought it was. You've demonstrated that at least one credible alternative exists. Now you will present a sketch of history that reveals the influence of the Reformers on this issue.

THE REFORMERS DISAGREED ON BAPTISM

By investigating the writings of the Church Fathers, we found out that baptismal regeneration—not symbolic-only baptism—was the universal belief of the Church for at least the first six centuries. When did the idea that baptism was only symbolic first appear? It turns out that it was not until the sixteenth century, when Ulrich Zwingli, one of the original Protestants, became the first Christian leader to seriously propose the doctrine. Interestingly, he still defended infant baptism as the proper way for a child to enter the Church and the covenant, but he rejected the Catholic teaching that God gave grace through baptism and that the sacrament regenerated the person. Zwingli opined: "In this matter of baptism—if I may be pardoned for saying it—I can only conclude that all the doctors have been in error from the time of the apostles. . . . All the doctors have ascribed to the water a power which it does not have and the holy apostles did not teach."[14] Zwingli was a Swiss Catholic priest who in the early 1500s wanted to reform the Church, especially the morals of the clergy and the people. But along the way he came up with novel opinions about Christian truth, and like Martin Luther began teaching his version of Christianity against the Church's doctrines. In addition to coming up with the new doctrine that baptism does not regenerate, but only serves as a tangible "seal" that one has already been forgiven by God, Zwingli proposed the idea that the Eucharist was purely symbolic. With these novel opinions he clashed not only with the Church but with other Reformers.

Zwingli became one of the most important figures in the early Reformation, though today his popularity is dwarfed by Luther and John Calvin. Still, his influence on the beliefs of many Protestants, including Evangelicals, has been tremendous. Most Protestants' beliefs on baptism today derive from those of Zwingli or Calvin (who took a middle road between

---

14. Huldrych Zwingli, "On Baptism," Zwingli and Bullinger, in The Library of Christian Classics, Vol. 24, Edited by G.W. Bromiley, p. 130.

Luther and Zwingli): baptism is important—even very important—but ultimately only a symbol.

CRAFTING THE ARGUMENT

Present this historical evidence to your friend, and, when the time is right, continue with the following line of argument. Let's assume for a moment that Zwingli and the Anabaptists were correct in saying that baptism is only symbolic. What consequences does that lead to?

First, it means that the Church went off the rails from the beginning of its existence by teaching baptismal regeneration from the time of the apostolic Fathers. It also means that every Christian up until the sixteenth century failed to interpret the Bible correctly on baptism. In spite of the alleged clarity of the Scriptures on this issue, all those faithful Christians couldn't see the obvious.

If the leadership of the second-century Church did indeed fall into serious heresy over this essential doctrine (on which the salvation of millions

ROCKY SHOAL: CATHOLICISM IS TOO POLITICALLY LIBERAL

Your Protestant friend says: "Catholics have voted for so many liberal politicians, men and women who have promoted euthanasia, embryo-destructive stem–cell research, abortion, and same-sex 'marriage', among other evils. They find justification for these voting decisions in Catholicism's labyrinthine rules."

In response, you can point out that:

- The Catholic Church is neither right nor left, in the Western political sense
- The Catholic Church teaches principles that should be applied to a Catholic's decision about whom to vote for
- Sadly, many Catholics have ignored these principles and voted for candidates who endorsed many intrinsic evils (e.g., abortion) without valid justification
- Catholic social teaching is rich and deep, and sometimes none of the candidates faithfully conform to it, but in such cases oftentimes one candidate is clearly better (or less bad) than the others

could depend) how can we have confidence in the books that those same heretical Church leaders selected for the canon of the New Testament? There is no principled reason to believe that the Church got baptismal regeneration wrong but the New Testament right.

Ask your friend how likely he thinks it is that a Swiss man who lived 1,500 years after Christ was the first to finally get the doctrine of baptism (and on Eucharist for that matter) right.[15] Most honest people would admit it's not likely. You can point out how similar this is to the Mormon claim that after eighteen centuries Joseph Smith finally discovered true Christianity. If Zwingli was right, it means the Holy Spirit failed to do what Jesus said he would do in John 16:13: "When the Spirit of truth comes, he will guide you into all the truth." We know that Christ's promises are true, so the Holy Spirit did not fail to lead the Church into the truth.

SELECTIVE AGREEMENT WITH THE REFORMERS

A good point on which to close out this subject is the doctrine of infant baptism. There's a good chance that your friend rejects it. If he is a Protestant of the Evangelical, "Bible Christian," nondenominational, or Pentecostal varieties, he holds to believer-baptism (also called credobaptism). You can point out to him that Zwingli, from whom he received his belief in symbolic-only baptism, held firmly to infant baptism[16] and argued vehemently against the Anabaptists, who rejected it. He even put Anabaptist leaders to death for teaching credobaptism! Why then should your friend look to him as a cred-

---

15. Some Protestants have latched onto the fantasy that a tiny remnant of "true Christians"—Protestant in belief—existed for these 1,500 years, living in mountain caves or hidden villages perhaps, passing on the "true faith" to their progeny. It's a nice idea but has no evidence demonstrating it.
16. *Baptism, Rebaptism, and Infant Baptism*, Huldrych Zwingli.

ible interpreter of the Bible on one baptism doctrine when he made such a serious error on another? The same goes for Calvin and Luther, both of whom also taught infant baptism.

It's not just on infant baptism that your friend is likely in conflict with the Reformers. Zwingli and the other Reformers believed in many Catholic Marian dogmas as well. Luther believed in the Immaculate Conception. Zwingli and Luther both believed in Mary's perpetual virginity (Calvin was neutral-to-sympathetic on this doctrine). Virtually no Protestants today believe these doctrines are biblical. They would consider anyone who believes them to be in serious error, or perhaps not even true Christians, and would approach anything else they believed or taught with great skepticism. So why, then, do they unquestioningly hold to the tradition of the Reformers when it comes to baptism?

Your goal here is to help your friend see where his beliefs come from. They're not simply the result of reading the clear meaning of Scripture for what it is; rather they are centuries-old traditions that they received from teachers and pastors who ultimately trace them back to the novel doctrines of the Reformers. This will not sit well with him, because he has always been under the impression that his beliefs come directly from a plain reading of the Bible. It's okay if he refuses to concede that his beliefs have been influenced by these men. It is a hard pill to swallow, and it may take time for him to do so.

Your work has been done simply by presenting to him this additional evidence on baptismal regeneration. You're continuing to drop small weights on the scale, and it may take time for him to recognize what they add up to.

By this time, your friend will probably be tired of playing defense. While researching your arguments, he has undoubtedly come across arguments against the Catholic Church that he wants you to answer. And it is only fair that you be willing to listen and respond to them. In the next section, we will look at some of the attacks on the Catholic Church he might come back with, and provide solid defenses against them. These include papal infallibility and the problem of immoral popes, Marian dogmas, the Crusades and the Inquisition, and the sexual abuse scandal.

But before we close out this section, you need to be equipped to begin understanding the wide variety of Protestants whom you may meet, in person or online. The next chapter provides vignettes of two particular types of Protestant and tells you how to deal with them.

YOUR PRAYER TOGETHER
"Father in heaven, we wish to know the truth about baptism and the Eucharist, for you established these actions and commanded us to do them. Lead us to your divine truth that we might believe and practice it with all our hearts."

READING RECOMMENDATIONS
• The "Marburg Colloquy" between Martin Luther and Ulrich Zwingli
• *Christianity's Dangerous Idea,* by Alister McGrath

11

TWO PROTESTANTS YOU WILL MEET

Honestly, being a Catholic apologist has its downsides. One is that people feel they can email you out of the blue with a list of arguments against the Catholic Church and then demand you respond. Over the years I've received many such emails, some rudely written, others genuinely seeking answers. One upside to these messages, though, is that they give me insight into a broad swath of Protestant Christians and the varied obstacles that they face. I have noticed that many of those Protestants resemble one of two types: the Certain Guy and the Robot.

THE HOLY SPIRIT CERTAINTY GUY

Charles was a Protestant who emailed me, describing something of his history as a Christian: going from one denomination to another many times over the years as his beliefs changed and he decided his current church was in error.

His meanderings had finally made him wonder if, perhaps, Catholicism was what it claimed to be. "Maybe there *is* a true Church?" he asked. When a Protestant comes to this question on his own, it is a wonderful thing. It indicates an openness to the possibility that the whole Protestant paradigm may be mistaken; instead maybe God did preserve the Church from error.

In the second half of his email, however, Charles listed his chief objections to Catholicism, notably the Church's beliefs about Mary. Charles ended by saying:

I am a Christian struggling with the dilemma of where to gather among other Christians to worship God—but the issue of praying to Mary is a stumbling block, or should I rather say, heresy in my opinion, which I regard as equal to idolatry and which will keep me very far away from the Roman Catholic Church.

Charles's candor was refreshing. He said very directly that he could not imagine becoming Catholic due to what he saw as heresy. In my response, I gently nudged him with questions about how he knew what Christ and the apostles taught and how he knew that his interpretation of Scripture was accurate. I also gave evidence for the perpetual virginity of Mary and the intercession of the saints. I kept it to a few paragraphs and waited for his response.

Charles opened his reply thanking me for my email, but then he said, "However, I am still completely unconvinced by your reasoning—and I know that I indeed do have the Holy Spirit who leads me into all truth and he is not leading me to believe what you have suggested."

Ah, there it was! He believed that he had the Holy Spirit and read John 16:13 to mean that the Spirit will lead him individually into all truth. He was sure that the Holy Spirit was showing him that I was in error and that he was not.

STRIKING AT THE ROOT

When you encounter the Certain Guy, you could respond to his impregnable certainty with an equally confident assertion, as I did: "I also have the Holy Spirit and am unconvinced by your reasoning, so we are at an impasse. Further, Martin Luther and John Calvin believed they had the Holy Spirit, and they rebutted other Protestants who held the same interpretation that you did about Mary's perpetual virginity. So our impasse deepens."

In this brief exchange we exposed the fundamental problem of Protestantism. He claims he's right because he has the Holy Spirit. I claim that I'm right for the same reason. And according to Protestantism, no person or church or institution can adjudicate our competing claims. In any dialogue with a Protestant it is important to reach this point, so that your friend can realize the unresolvable dilemma that his beliefs create.

Charles emailed back telling me that he "does not arrogantly pick and choose" his beliefs as I suggested. Of course, I never claimed that his choosing was done in arrogance, only that he was indeed picking and choosing: picking which issues were essential versus non-essential, and choosing what to believe on each of those issues. Even if he did not do it arrogantly, the fact remained that he was doing it, and that under Protestantism's paradigm he had no choice but to come up with an individual belief on every issue he came across.

It is instructive that even though I said nothing about him acting arrogantly or capriciously in choosing his beliefs, Charles inferred that I made such an accusation. Misunderstandings like this occur often in any discussion about beliefs. Faith abides deeply within us, and any perceived challenge to our beliefs can result in a defensive reaction, even if our discussion partner acts in a completely amiable way.

Our email exchange continued for a bit longer and wended toward the question of whether *sola scriptura* was true, but for our purposes here the main point has been shown. When you face Certain Guy, who is absolutely confident in his interpretation of Scripture and of the Holy Spirit's guidance, simply push back, without any rancor, that you can claim the same thing, and so reveal a conundrum.

THE ONE-WAY STREET

About six months after my book *The Protestant's Dilemma* was published, I received an email from a Protestant man (whom I'll call Louis) directing me to his website, where he was making a chapter-by-chapter rebuttal of my book. He was brief but respectful enough, so I went and checked it out. His was the first substantive attempt to rebut my arguments, so I was interested in what he had to say.

Unfortunately, his site had the look and feel of a Web 1.0, circa 1998 site hand-coded in basic html. Even though as a computer programmer I winced, I was able to ignore that, but since he was attempting a rebuttal one chapter at a time, I also had no way of knowing when he posted more updates for me to read.

I kindly emailed Louis and suggested he go with a standard blogging website, which would allow him to publish each of his rebuttal attempts as blog posts that I and others could subscribe to. He paid no attention to my suggestions and instead just kept sending me short emails, about once a day, that had a link in them to his argument web pages.

I figured that I would give him another chance to interact in a constructive way, so I went to one of his links, read his argument, then sent him an email rebutting the argument. In this particular case, he was denying that Mary was the mother of God. I explained why this title is valid, but he ignored my argument and sent me yet another link to his web page.

At that point I realized I was dealing with someone uninterested in interacting like a human being. Rather, like a machine he wanted to blast his arguments at me—whether they were sensible or not—and didn't want to have a discussion. It was a one-way street. I called him out on this and said I would automatically filter his emails into the trash if he continued this robotic behavior. He immediately continued it, and I filtered his emails. The next day he emailed me from a different address!

DOMO ARIGATO, MR. ROBOTO

Most Protestants, thankfully, are not robots like Louis. But some are, and possibly you will encounter one, whether virtually or in person. Keep in mind that you are not obligated to respond to them or to play by their (lopsided) rules. In my experience, interacting with such people goes nowhere, as they are not truly open to discussion and honest analysis of the arguments.

Instead, they are locked into existing beliefs that see Catholicism as apostate or heretical, and have one goal: to disseminate attacks against the Church in rapid-fire fashion.

And remember, even when people act in such exasperating ways, seek to forgive them. Pray for them—the best thing and often the only thing that you can do—and leave them in our Lord's hands. You hope to see them and be with them in heaven one day, in spite of their errors and your own faults and weaknesses.

READING RECOMMENDATIONS
Surprised By Truth series, by Patrick Madrid

PART III

SURVIVING THE RAPIDS

12

THE POPE PROBLEM

THE PAPACY IS a keystone of the Catholic Church. If Protestants could disprove papal infallibility or Petrine succession, they could disprove Catholicism. Protestants since Martin Luther have recognized this fact and, unsurprisingly, sought to discredit and undermine the Catholic doctrines surrounding the bishop of Rome. If you need a hill to die on in defense of Catholicism, this is it.

Your job is to meet every accusation and attack with a careful defense and riposte. Your friend will inevitably bring up arguments against the Church related to the papacy. Far from shying away from discussing these issues, you should welcome the dialogue, for these arguments must be addressed before you friend will seriously consider the Catholic Church's claims.

Objections to the papacy generally fall under two categories: immoral popes and the dogma of papal infallibility.

IMMORAL POPES
Though relatively few in number, there *were* popes whose lives were anything but Christ-like. Pope Alexander VI was one of them. He reigned in the decades just prior to the Protestant Reformation, fathered illegitimate children while a cardinal, and generally seemed more interested in promoting his own

selfish interests than those of Christ's Church. As a Catholic, you need make no excuse for his behavior or the behavior of other popes who were worldly and lascivious. Instead, freely concede that there were immoral popes.

Now, your Protestant friend will likely follow up your concession with one of a few arguments. The first runs like this: "The Catholic Church relies on apostolic succession for its authority, but because immoral popes were links in that supposedly unbroken chain, they corrupted it and therefore broke it. So the Catholic Church's claim to authority today is invalid."

How do you respond? First, realize that this argument's premise is just an opinion that your friend proposes as true. In other words, who made the rule that the existence of immoral Church leaders must cause the authority Christ gave to the Church to disappear? The Church doesn't claim apostolic succession works this way. The Bible doesn't say that only morally impeccable people can serve as God's instruments; quite the contrary, Scripture is full of sinners whose moral failings didn't disqualify them from the Lord's service. So there's no reason to accept this premise without argument.

DONATISM CONDEMNED

Additionally, the Church did actually confront this question in the fourth century. The Donatists were a group of bishops who claimed that unfaithful bishops and priests prevented the graces of God from flowing into the members of the Church via the sacraments. For example, we know that God regenerates a person through baptism, but the Donatists taught that if the minister who performed the baptism was corrupt, unfaithful, or not personally orthodox, then the baptism itself was invalid. The baptized person was *not* reborn.

This teaching, if broadly adopted, would have had disastrous implications. Since it wasn't always possible to know whether the minister of sacraments was morally upright and faithful, no one would ever know for sure who was validly baptized and who was not, or whether the Eucharist one received was validly consecrated, truly changed into the body of Christ. The Church rejected this teaching as heresy, rightly affirming that the saving graces of God that came through the sacraments could not be conditioned upon some minimum level of clerical holiness.

Similarly, the authority God gave the Church through apostolic succession can't be conditioned on the personal holiness of the successors. How much immorality would it take to break the chain? Who gets to make that determination? And would faithful popes and bishops lose their authority because of unfaithful ones? No, if a certain degree of faithfulness were required of Christ's ministers, the Church would have lost its authority with the apostles, almost all of whom wavered in their faith, acted selfishly at times, and gave in to vanity, pride, and cowardice.

Instead, God instituted rightful leaders in his Church and made their authority substantially transferrable (apostle to bishop, then bishop to bishop). We see this line of authority in the Bible, when Matthias is chosen to succeed Judas Iscariot, as well as when Paul writes to Timothy and reminds him of his authority and the gift he received through the laying-on of hands (2 Tim. 1:16, 1 Tim. 4:14). We also see it in the earliest Christian writings, in St. Ignatius of Antioch's letters and in St. Clement's letter.[17] In no case is the transfer of authority,

17. First Epistle of Clement to the Corinthians, Chapters 42 and 44. St. Ignatius: Letter to the Ephesians, Chapters 3–6; Letter to the Trallians, Chapters 2, 3, and 7; Letter to the Magnesians, Chapters 2–4, 6, and 7. St. Ignatius's Letter to the Romans has a different tone than the others, remarkable in the deference he shows to the Church in Rome, a striking nod to the primacy of the bishop of Rome.

or the maintenance of that authority, conditioned on the faith or moral rectitude of the man to whom it's transferred.

So although it is true that, over the centuries, some faithless and immoral men managed to become bishops and even popes, this fact has not prevented God from preserving the authority he gave to his Church.

If it had, think of the pitiable state we would be in today. We would have no way of knowing what were authentic expressions of the deposit of faith, versus mere fallible human opinions. The canon of Scripture would be up for grabs, as would the correct interpretation of Scripture on every single doctrine. We would be divided over almost every moral and theological issue imaginable, as one person raised up his own opinion against another.

In short, it would look a lot like Protestantism does today: endless factions and denominations and men all claiming that they are speaking the truth. In Protestantism, without an unbroken chain of apostolic authority to provide trustworthy guidance, there is no principled way to distinguish what is the content of the Faith from mere human opinion about that content. Instead, the most charismatic or intelligent-sounding voice prevails, and sways the ever-confused throng to his fallible opinions, at least until someone more attractive arises. Orthodoxy is decided by which Protestant king happens to be on the throne, or by which Protestant pastor sells the most books.

PAPAL RECALL?

Some Protestants, especially in America, will voice a second complaint stemming from the existence of bad popes: there's no democratic way to remove them from power.

Although it is true that a Catholic cannot un-elect the pope, and that the Church is a not a democracy, it is also true that Catholics must only follow the teachings of the Church and not the bad personal example of any of its leaders who are immoral. You can remind your friend that Jesus said, "The scribes and the Pharisees sit on Moses' seat; therefore, do whatever they teach you and follow it; but do not do as they do, for they do not practice what they teach" (Matt. 23:2–3). The same can be said of the Catholic Church's leaders. They sit in rightful authority over the faithful, and because God has protected the teachings of the Church from error, we can follow them confidently. But when leaders do evil and don't follow the Church's teachings, we are obliged to *not* follow their actions.

Further, far from not being able to do or say something about such immorality, Catholics are encouraged to prudently and charitably speak up and denounce such behavior. In the fourteenth century, St. Catherine of Siena did just that. She was not afraid to rebuke popes whose actions were immoral or cowardly. She prayed for them, exhorted them, and at times upbraided them in hopes of winning their deeper conversion to Christ. The Church recognized her faithfulness and declared her to be a saint and also a Doctor of the Church (an eminent and reliable teacher of the Faith).

INCREDULITY OVER INFALLIBILITY

The Church teaches that the pope is infallible—protected by God from making an error—when he makes a binding decree on faith or morals intended to be held by the whole Church, and does so in his official capacity as shepherd of all Christians. Note that this is a *negative* protection—it does not mean that the pope will always and exhaustively say everything that is true about a given topic. It only applies to matters of faith and morals; to what Christians believe and how they should act. It doesn't protect a pope from teaching error about quantum physics!

Many Protestants confuse infallibility with *impeccability* and think that if a pope is immoral then infallibility is proven false. But this is not so. The definition of infallibility has never included a particular pope's moral behavior, only what he teaches under the conditions given above. In fact, it is a testimony to infallibility that none of the immoral popes ever taught error or reversed a dogma of the Church. This distinction is critical to make and to help your friend understand. Even when you present this information to him, expect to get resistance. Your explanation may sound to him like the Catholic Church is trying to weasel out of a loophole. Be patient and remind your friend that he must use the Church's definitions when trying to understand these matters, not definitions made up by others. And show him that those definitions are reasonable.

Your friend may object further that no one but God himself is infallible. It defies reason to say that any human being could be.

First, remind your friend that infallibility doesn't mean that popes are little gods, or that they have any special powers on their own, apart from what God gives them. Jesus sent out his disciples to do godlike things such as heal the sick and raise the dead (Matt. 10:8), but Protestants understand that they did so by Jesus' power, from his commission. Likewise, the gift of papal infallibility comes from Christ, and stems from his commission to the apostles—and specifically Peter (see Matt. 16:18-19, Luke 22:31-32, John 21:15-17)—to lead and teach his flock with surety.

You can agree with him that reason alone can't prove papal infallibility. Is that the test he wants to apply? After all, reason alone can't prove the Incarnation, or the Trinity, or many other doctrines of the Faith. But you *can* offer evidence that supports this teaching. For instance, point out that your friend's Bible contains two books written by St. Peter, who was the first bishop of Rome. Your friend most likely believes that God inspired Peter when he wrote these books. So what is the principled reason for believing that God infallibly inspired one bishop of Rome to write Scripture, but did not give any other bishops of Rome the (somewhat lesser) infallibility of not teaching error? Your friend needs to explain why he accepts a kind of infallibility in one case but not in another.

Furthermore, given the weakness and fallibility of humanity, it stands to reason that for Christ's Church to teach Christ's truth faithfully and accurately, God would provide a way to protect it from falling into error. His Church needed to have a visible head on earth, one person who could hold the keys to the door of the deposit of faith and prevent anything false from coming in to corrupt it. Jesus chose Peter for this role, in his office as bishop of Rome, and Peter's successors have continued in it. They have confirmed (or refused confirmation of) decrees proposed by ecumenical councils. They have spoken out to proclaim the truth when it was attacked. They have strengthened their brother bishops just as Peter did, and as Christ prophesied (see Luke 22:32). Without this visible head as the standard for unity and orthodoxy, this last judge of doctrine, the Church could not teach with authority and could not say whether anyone was in full communion with Christ's Church or in schism.

Your friend may try to argue that certain popes actually did teach heresy. Pope Honorius I is a favorite of Protestants in this regard. It's worth delving into Pope Honorius briefly. In the 600s, a new heresy arose called Monothelitism (that Christ had one will and not two). It was not truly a new heresy, but more of a "compromise" heresy to attempt to reconcile back to union Monophysite heretics.

Sergius, the Patriarch of Constantinople, wrote to Pope

Honorius inquiring about Monothelitism. Pope Honorius ideally would have responded with a clear affirmation of dyothelitism (two wills), nipping the nascent heresy in the bud, but he did not. He wrote a letter back to Sergius that was more political than theological in nature but, somewhat ambiguously, seemed to tacitly condone Monothelitism. Now, whether Pope Honorius was a Monothelite heretic or not has been debated for centuries. The weight of the evidence is against it. *But even if he were a Monothelite*, the letter he wrote to Sergius in no way was a formal teaching of the Roman pontiff intended to teach dogma for the whole Church.

From the First Vatican Council *Pastor Aeternus*:

> Therefore, faithfully adhering to the tradition received from the beginning of the Christian faith, to the glory of God our savior, for the exaltation of the Catholic religion and for the salvation of the Christian people, with the approval of the Sacred Council, we teach and define as a divinely revealed dogma that when the Roman Pontiff speaks *ex cathedra* [from the Chair of St. Peter], that is, when, in the exercise of his office as shepherd and teacher of all Christians, in virtue of his supreme apostolic authority, he defines a doctrine concerning faith or morals to be held by the whole Church, he possesses, by the divine assistance promised to him in blessed Peter, that infallibility which the divine Redeemer willed his Church to enjoy in defining doctrine concerning faith or morals.[18]

This letter of Pope Honorius to Sergius was about as far from an *ex cathedra* decree as one can get. So, while non-Catholics have tried to make hay out of Pope Honorius for cen-

18. *Pastor Aeternus*, 9.

turies, the letter favors the Catholic explanation heavily. It is telling that Honorius and a tiny few other cases are the best that Protestant apologists have come up with, in spite of having 2,000 years of grist for their mill.

WHAT ABOUT THE CLASSIC CATHOLIC PROOFTEXT OF MATTHEW 16?

Notice that we have not proactively brought up Matthew 16:18-19 to your friend in defense of papal infallibility. This is the powerful passage where Jesus says he will build the Church on Peter, the rock, and that the gates of hell will not prevail against it. He also says he will give Peter the keys to the kingdom of heaven, with the power to bind and loose.

It is not that you *shouldn't* bring up these verses—by all means feel free to do so—but in my experience they are not the best way to help your friend see the truth of papal infallibility. The arguments for the Catholic interpretation of these verses are well-known, and a Protestant can find lots of counter-arguments (of varying quality) to them. A back-and-forth ensues, with each side plying the arguments they have read, and in the end you are playing on Protestant turf, trading verse interpretations. The heart of the matter is who has been given the guidance and authority from God to interpret Scripture. Answering that question is what you are helping your friend do for himself throughout your entire discussion.

YOUR PRAYER TOGETHER
The Glory Be.

RECOMMENDED READING
• Pope Clement's *Letter to the Corinthians* 42:4-5, 44:1-3
• *The Eternal City: Rome and the Origins of Catholic Christianity*, by Taylor Marshall

13

CONTRARY
TO MARY

RANKING RIGHT UP there with the papacy is the obstacle that Marian dogmas present to Protestants. You must address these objections as effectively as you can to help your friend see that there is support for them even early on in the Church's history, but realize also that most people do not accept all the Marian dogmas until they decide to become Catholic. The reason for this is simple: though all the dogmas have implicit support in Scripture, only a few of them are explicitly affirmed in the Bible.

MOTHER OF GOD

The Church declares Mary to be the Mother of God. This title strikes Protestants as blasphemous, for how can God have a mother? Your first task is to clarify that this title does *not* mean Mary is the mother of Jesus in his eternal generation, nor is she the mother of God the Father or God the Holy Spirit. Quite simply, Mary is the mother of Jesus Christ, the second person of the Trinity, and since Jesus is God, Mary is the mother of God.

Explicit support for this doctrine exists in St. Luke's Gospel: "And when Elizabeth heard the greeting of Mary, the babe leaped in her womb; and Elizabeth was filled with the Holy Spirit and she exclaimed with a loud cry, 'Blessed are you among women, and blessed is the fruit of your womb! And why is this granted me, that the mother of my Lord should come to me?'" (Luke 1:41-43).

Of course, "mother of my Lord" means "the mother of God," since there is only one Lord. Do not let your friend lightly brush aside this fact. This passage's weight is further strengthened by the fact that it includes the rare phrase "filled with the Holy Spirit," indicating in a special way that what Elizabeth said was from God.

The title "Mother of God" is necessary. If it is rejected, as a heretic named Nestorius proposed in the fifth century, terrible damage is done to the understanding of Christ's divinity and his Incarnation. A mother is the mother of a *person*, and everyone agrees that Mary was the mother of the person known as Jesus Christ. If she is not the mother of God, then Jesus Christ must not be God. The humanity of Jesus must be somehow separate or aloof from the divinity of God the Son. God only appeared to take on flesh and blood; only a human died on the cross—not God. Clearly, the theological repercussions of Nestorius's view are disastrous. This is why the Church, in the ecumenical council

ROCKY SHOAL: THE CHURCH IS ANTI-WOMAN

Your Protestant friend says: "The Catholic Church refuses to ordain women, even though women can do all the functions that priests do, as many Protestant female pastors demonstrate."

In response, you can point out that:

- In Catholicism, the priesthood is not primarily about being able to do some action, but about a state of being

- The Catholic priest images Christ (who was male), and marries the Church (which has female typology)

- Christ ordained only male apostles, and through Sacred Tradition these men ordained male successors down through the centuries

- God's greatest creation, the Catholic Church teaches, is a woman: the Virgin Mary

of Ephesus in 431, condemned Nestorius's error and declared it dogma that Mary was the mother of God.

PERPETUAL VIRGINITY

The Catholic Church teaches that Mary remained a virgin her entire life. The Orthodox churches also believe this dogma. But Protestants reject it almost universally. This dichotomy of belief results quite simply from the clash between Sacred Tradition, on the one hand, and *sola scriptura* with its related doctrine of perspicuity on the other. The Tradition of the Church from the earliest times held that Mary was a virgin her entire life. This doctrine was affirmed in the fifth ecumenical council held in Constantinople in 553.[19] But many passages from the Bible appear to directly contradict it.

For instance, we often hear in the Gospels of Jesus' "brothers and sisters" (see Matt. 13:35 and Mark 3:31). Any English reader without knowledge of the Church's historical teachings or of ancient Greek would naturally interpret these verses to mean that Jesus must have had biological brothers and sisters. The Bible also mentions that Joseph and Mary had no relations "until" Jesus was born (see Matt. 1:25), which may seem to suggest that they did have relations after he was born. Now, there are arguments that explain how the language used in these verses doesn't necessarily mean what it seems to mean in English. Such arguments are certainly one way of arguing against the idea that Mary was not a virgin, but in my experience it is better to only briefly mention that the original language does not imply what the English trans-

---

19. Second Council of Constantinople, Capitula 2. Catholic Encyclopedia. Source: Translated by Henry Percival. From Nicene and Post-Nicene Fathers, Second Series, Vol. 14. Edited by Philip Schaff and Henry Wace. (Buffalo, NY: Christian Literature Publishing Co., 1900.) Revised and edited for New Advent by Kevin Knight. <http://www.newadvent.org/fathers/3812.htm>.

lation seems to imply.

A better tack to take is the commonsense route. Ask your Protestant friend why Jesus, when he was hanging on the cross, would give his mother into the care of John the apostle, if indeed he had siblings? It makes no sense; his mother would be under the care and protection of her own children and not an unrelated friend, no matter how close John might have been to her Son.

Next, share with your friend the historical fact that all of the great Protestant Reformers—Martin Luther, John Calvin, and Ulrich Zwingli—believed in the Perpetual Virginity of Mary. These were the champions and original proponents of *sola scriptura*, yet they knew that the Church had always believed in this doctrine and that the biblical passages Protestants today point to as contradicting it, in actuality, do not. The Reformers had no qualms about rejecting the Catholic Church's teachings, but they kept this one, which indicates that there were good reasons for them to do so.

Another factor behind Protestants' rejection of this dogma is their rejection of celibacy for the kingdom as a valid choice of vocation. Suggest to your friend that he read Matthew 19:1-12, where Jesus praises those who choose to renounce marriage for the sake of the kingdom, as well as 1 Corinthians 7, where St. Paul does the same. Catholics have treasured this calling as a gift from God, but sadly Protestants threw it out in their over-reaction against the Church during the Reformation. During your discussion of this topic, you are facing not only different interpretations of the Bible, but also a fundamental disagreement regarding Christian celibacy.

The fact that the Bible seems so clearly to contradict Mary's Perpetual Virginity provides more evidence that Scripture is not as easy to understand as most Protestants think it is. Surely if Mary had not remained a virgin, most Christians from the early Church would have spoken up and pointed out that the Gospels refer to Jesus' brothers and sisters, indicating Mary and Joseph had other children. Instead, the opposite is the case: Mary's Perpetual Virginity is strongly supported and then dogmatically affirmed in an ecumenical council during the early centuries of the Church.

IMMACULATE CONCEPTION

Now, with the dogma of Mary's Immaculate Conception, we're getting into the tough ones. This dogma states that God preserved Mary from the stain of original sin from the moment of her conception. There is no Bible verse that explicitly tells us this; rather, it is a doctrine found primarily in Sacred Tradition. A corollary to this dogma is the Catholic belief that Mary never committed an actual sin throughout the course of her entire life.

The most common objection that Protestants bring against this teaching is that it seems to contradict Romans 3:23: "all have sinned and fall short of the glory of God." Protestants believe that all people, except Jesus, are sinners. The idea that Mary was sinless, they argue, implies that she didn't need Jesus as her savior and that she is too much like God.

Respond to the verse from Romans by pointing out that Paul is stressing here that Jews and Gentiles alike are sinners, so the "all" is intended to mean "Jews and Gentiles without distinction" rather than "every person who has ever lived without exception." Another argument to raise is that many babies die before they reach the age of reason. Since these children cannot commit any actual sins, the verse in Romans cannot be saying that all humans, without exception, commit sins. Perhaps none of these arguments will convince your friend, but they are important to bring up nonetheless, for they show that his interpretation does not work in many cases.

A great analogy to use goes like this: there is a big pit in the middle of the road. You and I fell into it and needed Jesus to pick us up and save us from the pit. Mary, however, was about to fall into the pit, too, when Jesus, her Son, threw his arms around her and saved her from falling. Then he carried her over the pit so that she would not fall in. The pit, of course, represents sin. Jesus is our savior in both scenarios.

Finally, if you think it may be helpful, do an Internet search for "Church Fathers Immaculate Conception," and you will find loads of quotations from even the earliest Fathers attesting to Mary's purity, faithfulness, and constant obedience to God's will. These don't "prove" the dogma is true, but they do demonstrate that this belief was found very early in Christ's Church, even in the second and third centuries.

ASSUMPTION

This dogma states that Mary, at the completion of her earthly life, was brought ("assumed") into heaven by God. It is another doctrine that finds its main support in Sacred Tradition. No biblical verse explicitly states it.

Most Protestants argue that this doctrine isn't found in the Bible and so should not be believed. This is a manifestation of their belief in *sola scriptura*. One way to argue for Mary's Assumption is to point out that Elijah in the Old Testament was said to be carried by a chariot into heaven. If God brought Elijah to heaven, he could do the same for Mary. (Similarly, it seems that God brought Enoch into heaven as well.) At the very least, these examples provide food for thought for your Protestant friend.

This dogma is not "necessary" in the strict sense that the salvation of humanity would be threatened were it not true. However, it has been believed since ancient times, and the

Orthodox churches teach it as well (they call it "the Dormition of the Theotokos [God-bearer]"). The Assumption is another special privilege given by Jesus to his mother.

It is best not to fixate on these last two dogmas too much. Your friend will probably not be convinced of them through arguments alone. He will need first to come to believe that *sola scriptura* is false and that the Catholic Church is authoritative. But it always helps to demonstrate that there is historical and biblical evidence for these teachings.

THE PROTESTANT PIANO TEACHER

My friend Lucia, who is Catholic, has seven children. For the past four years, they've been taught piano lessons by a wonderful Protestant lady whom I'll call Margaret.

Lucia always wondered when matters of faith and Catholic-Protestant differences would come up with Margaret. And eventually they did, when one of her sons, who had just made his First Communion, exuberantly shared the news of this event with Margaret.

When the lesson that day ended, Margaret said to Lucia, "Do you mind if we talk for a moment?" Lucia feared what was coming. She was afraid that their relationship was going to be harmed by a religious discussion.

Margaret asked about confession to a priest, but then quickly transitioned to doubts about the Catholic teachings on the Virgin Mary. Margaret specifically brought up Mary's supposed sinlessness and her Immaculate Conception. Lucia did her best to answer—she explained the doctrines quite well, in fact—but it was clear that Margaret was not convinced, since in her mind the doctrines were not found in Scripture.

They ended their discussion amicably, each promising to share some resources that the other could examine. Lucia found good talks by Scott Hahn from Lighthouse Catholic Media and brought them to their next talk. She believed that Margaret would be quite surprised to hear a Catholic scholar explaining Scripture and how it supported Catholic teachings.

Margaret also brought something to their next meeting, a DVD about the evils of the Catholic Church. They exchanged materials and each agreed to consider what was presented in the other's offering. Lucia went home and watched the video: a sensationalistic production claiming that the Catholic Church was the whore of Babylon from Revelation, that the pope wore white because he thought he was God, that the Jesuits were a devilish society that conspired to kill Protestants wherever they could be found.

To say that Lucia was taken aback would be an understatement. She had given Margaret a calmly reasoned explanation of St. John's Gospel by a Presbyterian-minister-turned-Catholic-scholar. In exchange, Margaret gave her a diatribe making every wild claim imaginable against Catholicism.

Lucia called me and asked how she should respond to this. I asked her what she thought she should do. "Well, I don't think I even know how to answer half the accusations made in this video," Lucia said. "So I planned to say to Margaret: 'Okay, so let's assume this is all true. Which church should I be going to?'"

Bingo! That route is an excellent one. It takes the wind out of the Protestant sails, avoids fruitless debate about whose interpretation of the book of Revelation is correct (hint: there are practically as many interpretations of this book as there are Protestants), and refocuses the discussion on the foundational issue of authority.

"To whom shall we go?" St. Peter asked Jesus at the end of John 6. That is the question Lucia planned to ask Margaret. Let's say you're right: whom should I follow? Protestants typically answer this question by saying, "Easy, read your Bible each day and find a church that teaches straight from the Bible."

That's a perfect response, as you can then send the ship sailing back to the first chapters of this book and ask them: "How do we know which books belong in the Bible in the first place? How do I know my interpretation is correct? Or that yours is? How do I even know that your criteria for identifying a good church are the right criteria?"

Discussions with Protestants often start out on peripheral issues. They begin with accusations about the pope, or Mary, or the Crusades. But you can deftly steer the craft back to the core issues, the ones that have the best chance of helping you make progress toward the truth.

Margaret had great respect for Lucia: she saw how loving her family was, how well-behaved and courteous her sons were, and through years of interactions she finally felt comfortable enough to raise questions about Lucia's Catholic faith. Lucia was probably the only Catholic Margaret had ever met who read the Bible, who knew her Faith, and who lived it. Only because of Lucia's credible witness did Margaret become curious how she could be Catholic and believe such obviously false (to Margaret) teachings.

How did Margaret respond to the Scott Hahn materials, which included a book he co-wrote with his wife? She actually loved the Hahns and their enthusiasm and said that she believed they were born-again Christians, "just off a tiny bit."

She went on to say that she had studied Scripture for the past thirty years and constantly listened to radio stations explaining the meaning of the Bible. She also listened to recordings by all kinds of theologians and Messianic Rabbis who "know the Hebrew and Greek Scriptures."

This type of response is common from Protestants. They have studied the Bible and listened to lots of preachers for decades, and so believe that they are correctly interpreting Scripture. But Martin Luther, John Calvin, and countless other Protestants before them *also* studied the Bible for decades, also knew Hebrew and Greek (and knew it a good deal better in many cases than your average Protestant preacher), and also were earnest in their prayer and study. Yet, they all contradict one another on many doctrines.

Protestantism has demonstrated that neither decades of study nor knowledge of Hebrew and Greek is sufficient for coming to unity in the truth. Years of study do nothing to remedy the root cause of all Protestant divisions: the fact that the individual Protestant is his own ultimate interpretive authority.

Margaret's response is the exact reason why Lucia should avoid going blow-for-blow in interpreting individual verses and passages of the Bible. Scott Hahn, a former Presbyterian minister, couldn't convince Margaret her interpretation was in error, and his knowledge is vastly greater than hers. Lucia should guide the topic back to the root of the tree.

YOUR PRAYER TOGETHER
Ask your friend if he is willing to pray a Hail Mary with you.

RECOMMENDED READING
• Luke chapter 1, Matthew chapter 19
• *Behold Your Mother,* by Tim Staples

14

MEDIEVAL MADNESS: THE CRUSADES AND INQUISITION

MOST OF MY Evangelical Protestant friends never bring up the Crusades. But some liberal Protestant friends of mine have. These Protestants either lean toward pacifism or have been formed by secular history texts and pseudo-historical television programs.

I recently read an award-winning children's book covering medieval times that devoted two pages to mischaracterizing the Crusades as brutal wars started by Christians against innocent Muslims. It is unsurprising then that the average American knows nothing about the Crusades, but has the firm impression that they were something bad, and in particular that it was "those Catholics"—or Christians in general—who were to blame. So you should be prepared to understand the basics about the Crusades in case your friend mentions the topic.

PROTESTANT PROPAGANDA

When the Protestant Reformers broke in schism from the Catholic Church in the sixteenth century, they attacked the Crusades and caricatured the Catholics who had taken part in them. Since the Crusades were called by the pope and therefore an example of papal authority and the unifying role of the bishop of Rome, the first Protestants wanted to do whatever they could to undermine them.

Your friend almost certainly knows very little about the Crusades. But he has heard that the popes ordered them, and to our modern minds, this seems wrong. A religious leader should keep himself separate from affairs of the State. This seems like common sense to us today, but in history it is a relatively recent phenomenon. During the time of the Crusades, religious leaders were often also civil leaders, and this included the pope. Indeed, the pope was the one leader who could unite (a very divided) Christendom behind the noble intention of making Jerusalem accessible to Christians and protecting the holy sites there.

Catholics also received indulgences for participating in a Crusade, the same indulgences that Martin Luther railed against when he began his protest of the Church. By this association, Luther thus opposed the Crusades and even believed the Muslim Turks to be God's divine justice against the Catholic Church. Not until the Turks arrived at Vienna in 1529 did Luther call for a Catholic and Protestant defense against Islamic aggression.

NOBLE PURPOSES

Before you can help your friend understand what the Crusades were all about, it's important that you have a basic understanding yourself. This can prove difficult in an age in which the secular mainstream has successfully waged a war of propaganda against the Crusades, leading to the widespread notion that they were greed-driven acts of Christian aggression against peaceful Muslim peoples.

Quite simply, the Crusades were a set of expeditions, undertaken over the course of several centuries, to win back the

Holy Land from Muslim forces that had invaded and conquered them.

From the first centuries of Christianity, Christians desired
to visit Jerusalem and see the places where Jesus had lived.
Many set off on pilgrimages that in some cases took years to
complete. But after the advent of Islam in the seventh century, these pilgrimages became more difficult and dangerous as
Muslims had conquered Jerusalem. Over the next four centuries, some of the Muslim leaders were relatively tolerant of
Christian pilgrims, but others were less so. In the eleventh
century a violent caliph named al-Hakim ordered the de-
struction of the Church of the Holy Sepulcher and the perse-
cution of all non-Muslims (including Christians).

Then the Seljuk Turks came to power, murdering priests
and pilgrims en route to the Holy Land. In 1065, a group of
12,000 pilgrims were about to reach Jerusalem when they
were slaughtered by the Seljuk Turks. In response to this bru-
tality and unrelenting Islamic aggression, Pope Blessed Urban
II in 1095 called for the first Crusade to liberate Jerusalem
and defend Christendom against Islam. Those who took up
the cross to go on armed pilgrimage with the Crusade would
do so for penitential purposes and not for money or fame.

As with all such militaristic ventures, the men who took sol-
emn vows to go on crusade had diverse degrees of virtue and
purity of motivation. Many had truly pious intentions spring-
ing from their Christian faith. Some had little faith and were
more interested in fame and fortune. Others went along for the
sheer adventure of it. For the most part, the Crusaders focused
on fighting the Muslims and winning back the Holy Land. But
it is also true that sometimes the baser among them did evil
things along the way. Sometimes they fought against one another; other times, shamefully, they attacked fellow Christians.
And yes, on a few occasions they killed Muslim innocents.

To help your friend see the Crusades in a better light, it's important to get across two main points.

The first is that the Crusades were not wars of aggression, but a response to aggression. By the time of the First Crusade in 1096, Muslims had waged continual war against Christendom since Islam began, conquering entire Christian nations from Africa to Spain. Later they would conquer Constantinople, the greatest Christian city in the world at the time, and threaten all of Europe. Most of the lands conquered and subjugated by Islam in North Africa and the Middle East remain Muslim to this day, and only the reconquest of Spain, along with dramatic stands against Muslim invaders in France, Austria, and the Balkans, kept Europe from being overrun as well. It's common today for the Crusades to be depicted as Christian invasions driven by religious intolerance and greed, but this depiction completely overlooks the brutal and unprovoked Muslim aggression that precipitated them, and the existential threat that Islam—first the Moors and then the Seljuk and Ottoman Turks—posed to Europe and to Christianity.

The second thing is that the primary motivation for the Crusades, which were first called for by Pope Urban II, was righteous zeal to return to Christian hands the most holy places on the planet. These were the places where Christ lived and died, where his apostles first taught, where his mother was laid to rest. And of course, they were many of the places where the history of the Old Testament played out, too. These places are, or should be, precious to Protestants, too. Most of them understand that the things of God are worth fighting for—especially to keep from being despoiled by unbelievers.

Indeed, the patrimony of the Crusades and of Christendom belongs to Catholics and Protestants alike. It is convenient for Protestants to distance themselves from the bad things that occurred in Christian history (attributing those unfortunate events to the Catholics) while associating the good events with their own faith, but it is not honest to do so. If not for the Catholic Crusaders, most especially Don Juan of Austria, sometimes called the "last crusader," who heroically led the Holy League Catholic armada in a miraculous defeat of the larger Turkish fleet in 1571 at Lepanto, Europe would have been overrun and conquered by Islam.

A good idea for discussing the Crusades with your friend is to admit that you do not know much about them. Each crusade had different aims, different highlights and low points. Covering even one of them in any depth takes hours of study. So invite your friend to read about the Crusades together with you. Don't be surprised if he refuses to take you up on the offer, but if he does, you will both learn a lot and have much to discuss.

The Crusades are a great example of one of those peripheral topics that isn't a matter of theology or even a central issue dividing Catholics and Protestants, but which often must still be dealt with if your friend is going to make it all the way across the Tiber. Once he understands them better, his bias against the Catholic Church will diminish. And that is another small step toward achieving full communion.

THE INQUISITION

Along with the Crusades, the Inquisition is often the second part of a historical one-two punch that some Protestants like to throw at the Church. The Inquisition is much more likely than the Crusades to rub Evangelicals the wrong way. To them, the Inquisition was a tool to persecute Protestants (and proto-Protestants), silencing them so that the Catholic Church could keep its stranglehold on Christianity.

Having a ready defense for the Inquisition is thus even

more important than for the Crusades. You need to show your friend that he has likely imbibed several myths about them—how many people were actually killed for instance—and also that his understanding of the time period is anachronistic.

Since it's possible that your friend has a particularly jaundiced view of the Inquisition, it's best to tread carefully. For starters, you should simply ask him what he thinks the Inquisition was. Then ask what he thinks it proves about the Catholic Church. Most likely, he will answer that through the Inquisition's ecclesiastical courts the Catholic Church executed tens of thousands to millions of heretics, demonstrating that the Catholic Church is oppressive and evil, not allowing people free thought and religious choice.

SETTING THE RECORD STRAIGHT

Your goal here is one of education and gentle correction. The Inquisition—a broad term for a number of regional inquisitions over a long period during the Middle Ages—did consist of ecclesiastical courts that investigated and tried people for religious offenses. And yes, some of those people were then put to death by the state. But the numbers are wildly exaggerated in both the secular and Protestant imagination. No one knows exactly how many people were executed via the Inquisition, but the best historians agree that the number is in the thousands, probably not even reaching 10,000—certainly not millions or even hundreds of thousands.[20] This will not immediately change your friend's opinion of the Inquisition, but establishing that it was nowhere near as bloody as popularly claimed is important groundwork.

Many Protestants, especially Americans, are so used to separation of church and state that they can't imagine heresy be-

20. http://en.wikipedia.org/wiki/Spanish_Inquisition.

ing treated as a criminal offense. You can remind your friend that during the centuries in which the Inquisition operated, religious belief was considered not just a private ecclesial matter but something that affected society as a whole.[21] Egregious heresy could pose a danger to the public order. Consequently, church and state sometimes worked together—not just in Catholic countries but, after the Reformation, in Protestant ones too—to root out such dangers.

One group of heretics called the Cathars, for instance, arose in France in the twelfth century. They believed that the material world was evil, claimed it was created not by God but by an evil being who was equal and comparable to God. God himself was pure spirit, they asserted, so they denied that Jesus Christ could be God incarnate.

Further, the Cathars were aggressively opposed to the sacraments (including marriage), Church authority, the feudal government (by refusing to take oaths), and they promoted ritual suicide. Obviously, such beliefs are completely incompatible with Church doctrine, and they posed a threat to the stability of society. Catharism and Christianity could not peacefully coexist (nor would this have been a good thing even if possible, given the grave errors of this heresy). The Inquisition was one way in which France and the Church stamped out Catharism and restored public order, but the Church also tried reconciling them back to the true Faith through pastoral means such as sending missionaries like St. Bernard of Clairvaux and St. Dominic.[22]

It is important to point out that the question of the Inquisi-

---

21. See 2 John 1:7–11 for St. John's warning about a particular class of heretic and how they should not be welcomed or accepted in by Christians, lest disorder and evil arise.
22. http://en.wikipedia.org/wiki/Catharism.

tion concerns *disciplinary* matters in the Church and does not touch anything of the Church's doctrine. Your friend may try to argue that the Inquisition calls into question the Church's infallibility, but this is simply not the case. The Church since the very beginning has had to deal with heresies and those who promote them. The ways, whether good or bad, that it did this never affected the Church's dogmas one way or the other—they were merely the means by which the Church has enforced canonical penalties. Sometimes Church leaders wrongly disciplined people—it happened and still happens today—but that fact does not impugn the Church's infallibility, which only covers its teachings on matters of faith and morals.

Another consideration to bring up is that the means used by the Inquisition, which occasionally did result in execution by the state and a limited form of torture, were methods common to the larger civilization at the time. Western society today has little appetite for such means, but it would be wrong of us to impose that modern standard back onto history. And besides, even in its use of such means the Inquisition was generally temperate, merciful, and legally fastidious—usually much more so than the secular courts.[23] Its purpose was not to cause suffering but to bring people back into communion with the Faith.

If your friend comes from a Reformed tradition, it bears

<hr />

23. See the short account at http://www.catholicapologetics.info/apologetics/prot-estantism/holinquisit.htm, which describes Pope Gregory IX's work with the Inquisition to counter-act the unjust practices of retribution which secular authorities were inflicting upon people they deemed "heretics," as well as the mob rule that could take the law into its own hands and kill a supposed heretic. The judges of the Inquisition were chosen carefully, the accused were given a grace period to profess their orthodoxy, leniency was the rule rather than the exception, and the goal was the return of the person to full communion with the Church.

mentioning that the early Protestants did not hesitate to use coercion and even impose capital punishment on those who disagreed with them. Philip Schaff, the respected Protestant historian, wrote:

> To the great humiliation of the Protestant churches, religious intolerance and even persecution unto death were continued long after the Reformation. In Geneva the pernicious theory was put into practice by state and church, even to the use of torture and the admission of the testimony of children against their parents, and with the sanction of [Protestant Reformer John] Calvin. Bullinger, in the second Helvetic Confession, announced the principle that heresy could be punished like murder or treason.[24]

The first Protestants sometimes executed those who disagreed with them, even fellow Protestants. In England, after Henry VIII broke from the Catholic Church and especially during the reign of his daughter Elizabeth I, countless Catholic priests and laypeople were arrested, tortured, and executed, their lands and property confiscated by the state. During this period, priests risked their lives to minister to the "recusant" Catholics who refused to assent to the new Protestant religion. And so if historically using force to quell perceived heresy makes for false Christianity, then not only Catholicism but Protestantism must be rejected as false.

All this said, whatever abuses that were committed by the Inquisition should not be excused. Ideally the ecclesiastical judges would always have been holy men, wise and concerned with the salvation of the defendant's soul. And this was the case the vast majority of the time. But sometimes it

24. http://www.ccel.org/s/schaff/history/About.htm.

was not, and human prejudices overrode authentic Christian judgment. But as with the Crusades, the sins of some do not make the whole Inquisition an evil thing, or still less invalidate the truth of Catholic teachings.

Indeed, though it's important to discuss if your friend brings it up, the Inquisition is a peripheral issue to the central questions of authority between you and your Protestant friend. As soon as you can, try to move past it to more essential topics, ones that bear directly on the decision to be Protestant or Catholic. Do your best to quickly dispel the vague propaganda that your friend has no doubt heard and uncritically accepted, and then suggest moving forward to the next discussion.

YOUR PRAYER TOGETHER
The Divine Mercy chaplet.

RECOMMENDED READING
• "The First Crusade," *Catholic Encyclopedia*[25]
• *The Glory of the Crusades*, by Steve Weidenkopf

25. http://www.newadvent.org/cathen/04543c.htm.

15

THE "PAGAN SUPERSTITION" OF CATHOLIC WORSHIP

FEW ASPECTS OF Catholicism disturb Evangelicals more than the Mass, sacramentals, and distinctively Catholic prayers. During discussions with your Protestant friend, it is probable that he has brought up some obstacle surrounding these things.

"You re-crucify Jesus every Mass!" is a common accusation. The art, incense, and sacramentals—holy water, scapulars, relics of the saints—of Catholic worship confirm your friend's fears that Catholicism is warmed-over paganism and superstition. Catholic prayers and devotions such as the Rosary also offend Protestants, who believe them to violate the Lord's admonition to avoid babbling and repetition in prayer (Matt. 6:7).

MASSIVELY BEWILDERING

I recall, during my Baptist days, visiting a Catholic parish in my area. I had been invited to Mass by my Catholic friend for the first time. I watched as he dipped his fingers in the holy water font and made the sign of the cross. He encouraged me to do the same, but I politely declined. I didn't know what the holy water was supposed to mean, and I had never made the sign of the cross.

During Mass, I felt confused and out of place as the Catholics around me were sitting, then standing, then kneeling, then responding in unison or reciting a litany of words. I generally mimicked the motions but refused to kneel when everyone else knelt. For me, kneeling equated with worshiping. And I only worshiped God, not the priest or a statue or a piece of bread.

Mass did impress me in one aspect, however: it was full of Scripture. At many points I caught phrases and passages from the Psalms. The readings themselves were from the Bible. The words of the priest were the words that Christ said at the Last Supper. Regardless of whether Catholics were right or wrong, they definitely embraced a certain understanding of Sacred Scripture and attempted to follow it. But the whole experience was off-putting to me. I felt like a fish out of water amid dangerous tides of idolatry.

SHOULD YOU INVITE YOUR FRIEND TO MASS?

You *could* invite your Protestant friend to Mass. But in my experience it's not something you should do right at the beginning. The purpose of the Mass is not to evangelize non-Catholics. God can certainly accomplish that effect through it, and sometimes he does, but it can just as easily bewilder a Protestant and inadvertently deepen his misunderstandings. The Mass is a ritual: it doesn't come with instructions or explanations for the uninitiated.

Multiple times I have had friends tell me they invited their Protestant friends to Mass, only to forget that it was a Marian feast day of some kind, with the priest dedicating his entire homily to Mary and the prayers themselves tailored to asking the Blessed Virgin for her intercession. We as Catholics know that those are all good things, because we understand Mary's

ROCKY SHOAL: THE SEXUAL ABUSE SCANDAL

Your Protestant friend says: "The priest sexual abuse scandal, including the cover-ups by bishops, demonstrate that the Catholic Church is not guided by God and that priestly celibacy is evil."

In response, you can point out that:

• The sexual abuse scandal was evil (remember: agree where possible)

• The Church teaches that God protects its doctrines from error, not that he protects all its members from committing sins, even heinous ones

• Therefore the failure of these priests and bishops does not entail that the Catholic Church is false

• The accusation that priestly celibacy is a primary factor in the sexual abuse scandal is not supported by any data

• Sexual perversions take root long before the age that men enter the seminary

• Further, Jesus and St. Paul were both celibate, and both praised celibacy for the Kingdom (Matt. 19, 1 Cor. 7)

place at the service of her son and his Church. But Protestants who have no such grounding, and who may harbor fears of Catholic devotion toward Mary, can be repulsed further by what they wrongly perceive as idolatry.

Depending on the church you go to, there may be other pitfalls. During the Mass, Christ becomes present in the Eucharist and is given to us to consume. This is the source and summit of the Faith. The liturgy should therefore be celebrated with great reverence and adherence to the rubrics that the Church sets out. A reverently celebrated liturgy draws the heart and mind toward God, engages the senses, and most importantly reveals that something is going on here that is far deeper and more profound than a Protestant praise and worship session.

But many times the Mass is not reverently celebrated. A Mass with mediocre, non-sacred music, with a priest who is not being reverent or who is diverging from the rubrics, and

with the congregation acting
distracted and irreverent, may
disappoint your friend, or bore
him, or leave him thinking that
there's nothing really different
about Catholic worship after all.

A better invitation to ex-
tend to your friend might be to
RCIA, a Catholic Bible study,
a Theology on Tap event, or
some other type of introducto-

> • In the general population,
> most sexual abuse occurs
> within families, with married
> men being the perpetrators
>
> All that said, the Catholic
> Church should be held to a high-
> er standard, precisely because
> it is Christ's Church, and it is a
> scandal that these priests abused
> young people.

ry program. We have a course at our parish called *Jesus Is Lord*
that offers a semester-long introduction to Christianity, and
to Catholicism specifically. It is attended by both Catholics
and Protestants and is a great way to gently expose a friend to
the Catholic faith.

IS THE MASS BIBLICAL?

Whether or not your friend joins you for Mass, or has been to
Mass before on his own, he is bound to have problems with
it. He may object, for instance, that he cannot find the Mass
anywhere in the Bible.

A good way to respond to this accusation is to point out
that, first, the Bible simply does not tell us exactly *what* Christian worship should look like. This truth is proven by Protestants themselves, who have services that look wildly different—everything from austere worship gatherings to rock
concerts with a little prayer to high liturgical rites complete
with incense and vestments. In fact, differences in interpretation (and extrapolation) of the relatively few Bible verses on
the worship service are a frequent cause of Protestant churches splitting from one another. This reality is more evidence
against the perspicuity of Scripture.

That said, Scripture does give us some hints. The New Testament speaks of the disciples breaking bread together, singing psalms, and engaging in fellowship (see Acts 2:42–47). Jesus was recognized by the apostles on the Emmaus road when he broke the bread with them (cf. Luke 24:35). Even in these simple passages we can see evidence for the Catholic liturgy. Much deeper evidence exists, however, throughout the Bible and especially in the New Testament. For instance, the motif of the sacrificial lamb is found from Genesis to Revelation, from Abel's acceptable sacrifice to the lambs eaten during the Passover, from the bread and wine offered by Melchizedek to Abraham's sacrifice. Whole books have been written on this subject, solid Catholic books which I cannot recommend highly enough. Refer to the recommended readings at the end of this chapter if you want to go deeper on just how biblical the Mass is.

A WIND FROM THE EAST

You have another arrow in your quiver, however, when defending the Mass. And this from an unlikely source: the Orthodox churches. Various groups split from the Catholic Church over the centuries; included in those groups are Oriental Orthodox Churches and the Eastern Orthodox Churches. These churches retained valid apostolic succession and sacraments, and ancient traditions of belief and worship going back to the very earliest days of Christianity. For example, the Coptic Church, which broke in schism from the Church in the 400s, looks and believes very similarly to the Catholic Church. Its "worship service" is the Divine Liturgy, which resembles closely Eastern Catholic liturgies, as well as the liturgies of Eastern Orthodoxy. These liturgies are divided into distinct parts in the same way—with the Liturgy of the Catechumens allowing non-baptized to participate and the

Liturgy of the Faithful—and the parts contain substantially similar subdivisions: the Kyrie, antiphons, readings from the Bible, psalms sung, and the gospel proclaimed, with a homily to follow and then the celebration of the Eucharist (which all these Churches believe to be Christ really present).

The Coptic Church also recognizes seven sacraments, apostolic succession, the intercession of the saints, the veneration of Mary, prayers for the faithful departed, the real presence of Christ in the Eucharist, and many other ancient doctrines.

In short, the Coptic Church is light years closer to Catholicism than it is to Protestantism. And so if a Protestant wishes to condemn Catholicism for what he considers to be superstitious or unbiblical in the Mass, then to be consistent he must condemn the Copts, and the Orthodox, for those same things. No problem, your friend might say—they're all unbiblical and superstitious. Then you can ask him this: how is it that these different churches, even ones that broke in schism early on in Christian history, all worship in substantially similar ways though the New Testament does not describe these things in detail?

One possibility is that the Church became corrupted early on, across the entire world, in peculiarly the same way. If this theory were true, wherever the apostles planted churches and practiced the Faith they must have also transmitted corrupted liturgies that closely resembled one another, and that bore little resemblance to the vast majority of Protestant services that were to come many centuries later.

That's one possibility. Another possibility exists, however, one that is much more plausible and faithful to Scripture: These churches followed the Tradition of the apostles. That Tradition includes truths passed down and lived out, like the structure and content of the liturgy, like apostolic succession, like the number and meaning of the sacraments.

The New Testament, when interpreted in light of that Tradition, certainly supports these practices and beliefs, but you cannot point to a checklist of verses that prove them to be true, or even describe them in detail. The apostles left more than just the New Testament, though. They left their Tradition as lived out in the life of the Church: the office of bishop as successor to the apostles, the sacraments, the prayer life of the Church.

Without sitting him down for a detailed course on the history of the development of the liturgy, you can show your friend how the Coptic Church provides evidence that all these teachings, as well as the liturgical form of worship we recognize in Catholicism, were not Catholic "inventions" and accretions of the Middle Ages. They were beliefs and practices from early on, tracing their roots to the apostles themselves. They were found everywhere in the world where the Church had established itself. Hence, all the oldest churches have strikingly similar doctrines and forms of worship.

Few Protestants are familiar with even the populous Eastern Orthodox churches, so some education is often required when presenting this argument. But it is a powerful one, vindicating many ancient Christian practices that Protestants mistakenly believe to be peculiarly Catholic or medieval inventions.

YOUR PRAYER TOGETHER
The Liturgy of the Hours.

READING RECOMMENDATIONS
• *A Biblical Walk Through the Mass,* by Edward Sri
• *The Lamb's Supper,* by Scott Hahn

16

SALVATION FOR THE LOSING

MOST PROTESTANTS I have met do not believe you can lose your salvation. In other words, once someone has "prayed the prayer" or accepted Jesus into their heart or had a conversion experience, he is saved, no matter what else he may do in his life. Although exceptions exist, as they will among any group as diverse as Protestant Christians are, most maintain that salvation cannot be lost. This is based on one of two different beliefs: eternal security ("once saved, always saved") and predestination. Catholics, on the other hand, admit that someone can lose his salvation. Let's be more precise about what this phrase means. If one "lost" his salvation, it would denote that at one time he was justified by Jesus Christ and then at some point afterward became unjustified again. He was righteous before God for a time but then became unrighteous. This rubs against the Protestant grain, because justification is accomplished by having Christ's perfect righteousness *imputed* or credited to you. It's like a bank transaction or court verdict: once it's done, it's done. No double jeopardy. Before we understand the Catholic response to this, let's look closer at the two rationales Protestants use for defending their belief that salvation cannot be lost.

ONCE SAVED ALWAYS SAVED AND PREDESTINATION

Baptists, nondenominational Evangelicals, and various other Protestant communities believe that once you ask Jesus into your heart as Lord and Savior, repenting of your sins, you are eternally saved, and nothing you subsequently do can cause you to be damned. This is the meaning of "once saved always saved." They base their assurance on erroneous interpretations of several different verses, including this one from 1 John 5:13: "I write these things to you who believe in the name of the Son of God, so that you may know that you have eternal life." For these Protestants, this verse is a slam-dunk prooftext, because they interpret "know" to mean "indubitable knowledge."

But the Greek word for "know" in that verse[26] does not necessarily denote absolute certainty. In this context it means having confidence in being saved. That confidence is placed in God and is fully compatible with the Catholic doctrine that we have a confident hope in salvation, but not metaphysical certainty.[27] The Catholic teaching is compatible with the whole of the New Testament, where many verses place conditional requirements on forgiveness and salvation.[28]

Presbyterians, Reformed Protestants, and other Calvinists also believe you cannot lose your salvation, but they stress predestination as the reason for it. God is omnipotent, so he already knows who will be saved and who won't. Further, from the New Testament we know that only those the Father draws will come to Christ—these are his sheep, who hear his voice—and so God has elected some people (but not others)

---

26. Gk. *eideitei*.
27. John. 5:13, Romans. 8:38–39, among others
28. 1 Jn. 1:8–9; 1 Jn. 2:24–25; 1 Cor. 15:1–2; Col. 1:21–23; and many more. Jesus himself said we would not be forgiven unless we forgave the sins of others in Matt. 6:15.

to justification and then to perseverance in his grace. Everyone who is elected to initial justification will also be predestined to persevere in the faith, so their salvation is sure. Now, they may or may not know that they are one of the elect, so it behooves them to strive to faithfully follow Christ and his teachings, but nonetheless, how they live has no impact on their salvation. If they're of the elect, they're in no matter what, and if they aren't, hell awaits.

Both groups deal with apparent cases of apostasy, heresy, or grievous immorality among those who seemed to have been saved by saying that the person was never saved in the first place. Or, by assuming that such people are in fact saved and will return to following Jesus, even though they aren't now. It becomes a circular argument, and in practice means you can never, under either of these Protestant systems, know whether you or someone else is saved,

ROCKY SHOAL: CATHOLICS DRINK AND GAMBLE

Your Protestant friend says: "I see Catholics drinking alcohol—even getting drunk—and also gambling. These are stumbling blocks to weaker brothers at best, and strong temptations toward sin at worst."

In response, you can point out that:

- Nowhere does the Bible condemn drinking alcohol
- Getting drunk is a sin, and the Catholic Church teaches that
- If a Catholic knows he is around a recovering alcoholic (an example of a weaker brother), he may choose in prudence and consideration to abstain from drinking
- Gambling is not condemned in the Bible and amounts to a form of paid entertainment
- Gambling becomes a sin when one spends excessive money on it, depriving his family of necessary goods or charities of money that he committed to donate to

since many people appear to fall away at some point in their lives. Hence the very goal of the whole scheme—assurance of salvation—ends up being undermined. It doesn't matter if you feel saved now: at the end of your life you might sin and demonstrate that you actually never were.

CATHOLIC REALITY

The Catholic Church teaches that a Christian can indeed fall away from Christ and thus "lose" his salvation. Now, what that actually means is that he can leave the state of sanctifying grace, which you will recall means friendship with God. He can, by his actions, tell God that he doesn't want to be his friend anymore, that the Holy Spirit is not welcome in his soul. And God will respect this wish. He will not force himself on anyone. Love is only love if it is freely given. The good news is, Jesus constantly calls the person back, and if he repents and confesses his sins, God will return to dwell in him again, restoring him to friendship.

This doctrine scares the hell out of Protestants. And, one might say, it should. St. Paul said as much in Philippians 2:12: "Therefore, my beloved, as you have always obeyed, so now, not only as in my presence but much more in my absence, work out your own salvation with fear and trembling."

But more importantly these Protestants believe that this doctrine contradicts the gospel, because it seems to imply that salvation is dependent upon human actions rather than being solely dependent upon God's gracious action. If a Christian can *do* something that will cause him to become unjustified again, then salvation must somehow depend on human decisions and will, rather than on God alone. For the Baptist this is slightly less of a problem, since they admit some aspect of man's free will being involved in continuing to say yes to God (Arminianism). But for Calvinists this is anathema, since for them God predestines people to justification and perseverance in a monergistic way. Thus for a Calvinist it is nonsensical to speak of someone throwing a wrench into the divine works. It would potentially deny God's omniscience (as if he didn't know it would happen) and his omnipotence (as if he couldn't save someone without that person's help).

MAKE THE CATHOLIC CASE

In discussing this subject with your friend, be ready to present some verses from Scripture to support the Catholic teaching. None are perfect prooftexts, and, as we have seen, any interpretation you present to your Protestant friend will be contradicted or questioned, but that is fine. The point will be made that plausible interpretations of biblical passages exist that lend credence to the Church's doctrine. Start with the first part of John 15, where Jesus explains he is the vine and we the branches. Branches that do not bear fruit are cut off: they were once united to Christ the vine but are later cut off and thrown into the fire. Another good verse is 1 Timothy 4:1, that speaks of people abandoning or departing from the Faith. They were once believers but eventually rejected truth for lies and fell away.

Also, you may know people who were Christians, even for years or decades, but who now are not. I have a friend who meets this description. He believed for most of his life, until in his mid-20s when he decided that Christianity couldn't be true and became an agnostic. A good friend of mine, himself a Protestant pastor now, watched in grief as his Christian father left his mother for another woman, even though they had a Christian marriage of over two decades. The practical evidence is heavily in support of Christians being able to fall away.

Your friend may choose to go on the offensive, accusing Catholics of not having faith in God's saving power. But though that Catholics don't believe in Protestantism's "eternal security", we *can* have certain hope of eternal life because we believe in God's infinite mercy and power.[29] This hope is not contradicted by the possibility that we will at some point reject God and fall away. It is only opposed to despairing of one's salvation.

That said, certain hope does not mean *indubitable knowledge* that one is in a state of sanctifying grace or is predestined for heaven. The Council of Trent specifically forbade Catholics from making the presumptuous claim that they *knew* they would be saved:

> For as no pious person ought to doubt the mercy of God, the merit of Christ and the virtue and efficacy of the sacraments, so each one, when he considers himself and his own weakness and indisposition, may have fear and apprehension concerning his own grace, since no one can know with the certainty of faith, which cannot be subject to error, that he has obtained the grace of God.[30]

St. Joan of Arc, perhaps inspired by the Holy Spirit, gave the best answer when her ecclesiastical accusers attempted to trap her into admitting this type of presumption of her salvation when she said, "If I am not in the state of grace, may God put me there; and if I am, may God so keep me."[31] Humble yet hopeful: that's the Catholic position.

Many Protestants will not initially "buy" this reasoning. It will not seem to them the same as the assurance of salvation that they think they have. That's okay. Once again you are

---

29. See this article for a great explanation of assurance of hope along with references to Aquinas' *Summa Theologiae* http://www.calledtocommunion.com/2009/08/st-thomas-aquinas-on-assurance-of-salvation/.
30. The Council of Trent, Session VI, Chapter XI. http://www.ewtn.com/library/councils/trent6.htm.
31. From the records of her trial in the third public examination..

planting a seed. The fact is that Catholics have a confident hope, one that trusts in the mercy and love of God, and that is the proper assurance God has given us.

YOUR PRAYER TOGETHER
Act of Abandonment to Divine Providence, by St. Jane Frances de Chantal.

RECOMMENDED READING
• The Council of Trent, Session VI, Chapter XI[32]
• *What Must I Do to Be Saved?*, by Marcus Grodi

32. http://www.ewtn.com/library/councils/trent6.htm.

17

CONTRACEPTION
AND DIVORCE

NOT EVERY OBSTACLE you will encounter with your friend will be about something theological. For many Protestants, Catholic teaching against contraception and against divorce and remarriage represent irreconcilable differences between the Church and their conscience.

My parents are divorced. My three best friends from childhood all had divorced parents. For me and for many, divorce is a reality of life that is all too familiar.

But in the beginning it was not so. These words of Christ should strike us with their full force. We know from the Bible that the Israelites also had a way for a husband to divorce his wife, and that at the time of Jesus this practice was still going on. Yet Jesus taught that marriage was created by God to be indissoluble. The apostles were stunned by this teaching and murmured that perhaps it was better not to marry at all.

The Catholic Church is one of the last institutions that takes the indissolubility of Christian marriage seriously. It would be much easier if it did not. The entire annulment process, for instance, could be done away with, and Catholics could divorce and remarry as many times as they wanted, and for any reason. In other words, you'd have Protestantism. Today, Protestants can generally divorce and remarry with impunity, though the more conservative congregations among them do still exert a moral pressure that frowns on divorce and remarriage.

AN EXCEPTION?

Yet even a cursory examination of the New Testament passages on marriage would indicate that Protestantism has gone off the rails in this regard. The lone instance where Jesus could be construed to give some type of qualification to the indissolubility of marriage is far from being a slam-dunk for the Protestant interpretation: "And I say to you: whoever divorces his wife, except for unchastity, and marries another, commits adultery" (Matt. 19:9). The word *porneia* is translated here as "unchastity," but many Protestant translations say "adultery." Both are inaccurate. Does this mean that if one spouse is unchaste and commits adultery, a marriage is dissolved?

No it does not. A Greek word for adultery exists,[33] but Jesus didn't use it. He used *porneia*, and he used it to mean illicit or invalid. The Jewish audience of St. Matthew's Gospel knew that Jesus was referring to the illicit sexual relationships listed in Leviticus 18:6-18, in particular incestuous relationships (see 1 Cor. 5:1, where St. Paul also uses *porneia* with this meaning).

This interpretation harmonizes with the other Gospels, which emphatically say that "everyone" or "whoever" divorces their spouse and marries another, commits adultery.[34] Jesus is doing what He often did: teaching something radical. He was calling the people of God back to the original plan for marriage, and so He rebuked the Pharisees when they asked about the certificate of divorce that Moses allowed: "from the beginning it was not so" that a man would divorce his wife.

33. *Moicheia.*
34. Mark 10:11–12, Luke 16:18.

And in the New Covenant, the indissolubility of marriage would be another sacred truth restored.

Hence, the Catholic Church recognizes that it does not have the authority to separate what God has joined until death. The Church does not forbid civil divorce as such—there may be circumstances where it's practically necessary for a person to legally separate from his spouse (abuse, for instance). But if they were validly married to begin with, it's impossible for him to marry another while his spouse lives. Catholics who are legally divorced from their spouse and believe that for some reason their marital union was never validly effected may ask the Church to undertake an investigation of the circumstances of their marriage. This is the annulment process, and if it decides in favor of annulment, both spouses would be deemed free to "remarry"—though it wouldn't *really* be remarriage, since they were never married to each other in the first place.

UNFURL THE SAILS

In discussing this topic with Protestant friends, great tact is often necessary. Odds are good that they're divorced, have divorced parents, or have close friends and family members who are divorced. They may have loved ones who got married in the Catholic Church but then divorced and subsequently left, harboring bitterness. They themselves may be estranged from the Church because of a divorce somewhere on their family tree—or their own divorce.

It's essential, therefore, to present the teachings of the Church in a positive way. The writings of Pope St. John Paul II are fantastically helpful on this subject, in particular his theology of the body (see recommended reading selections at the end of this chapter). In the Vatican II document, *Gaudium et Spes,* the Church teaches that Jesus "implied a certain likeness between the union of the divine persons, and the unity of God's sons in truth and charity. This likeness reveals that man, who is the only creature on earth which God willed for itself, cannot fully find himself except through a sincere gift of himself" (24).

A husband makes a sincere gift of himself to his wife, and vice-versa. Each gives the gift and receives the gift of the other. The *Catechism* quotes from John Paul II's work *Familiaris Consortio* that delves more deeply into this beautiful truth:

> Conjugal love involves a totality, in which all the elements of the person enter - appeal of the body and instinct, power of feeling and affectivity, aspiration of the spirit and of will. It aims at a deeply personal unity, a unity that, beyond union in one flesh, leads to forming one heart and soul; it demands indissolubility and faithfulness in definitive mutual giving; and it is open to fertility. In a word it is a question of the normal characteristics of all natural conjugal love, but with a new significance which not only purifies and strengthens them, but raises them to the extent of making them the expression of specifically Christian values (CCC 1643).

The Catholic Church sees marriage as a profound union of man and woman, one where they ultimately form "one heart and soul." The Church has taken our Savior's words on marriage and the Sacred Tradition that he entrusted to it, and developed a piercing understanding of this sacrament.

Many Protestants view marriage highly and would agree it goes beyond a contract to the level of a covenant. But none have plumbed the depths of its mystery as has the Catholic Church. Present the Church's teachings in a winsome way and emphasize how faithful they are to Scripture. Point out

NAVIGATING THE TIBER

also that this is a case where those Protestants with a high view of marriage will have that respect elevated to an even loftier plane in embracing Catholicism. It truly is good news, a light for our dark world and the many broken marriages and families in it.

THE DANGEROUS SHOAL OF CONTRACEPTION

The Church's teachings on contraception become more comprehensible when illuminated by its teachings on marriage. For a person to make a sincere gift of himself in marriage, he must give himself fully and fruitfully. God made us with the ability to procreate new human life. When a person uses contraception, he attempts to thwart that gift. He seeks to close off the marital embrace from its procreative aspect, to have the pleasure of sexual union while avoiding the possibility of conceiving a child. Contraception is thus incompatible with making a sincere gift of oneself. It holds something back, one's fertility, and says in effect that "I give some part of myself to you, but not all of myself."

Contraception is a tricky subject to discuss with Protestants. Most Protestants have used or are using contraception. So when this topic arises, your Protestant friend may get defensive. In my discussions with Protestants on this subject, their first response is one of amazement that any modern person would think contraception is wrong. And after presenting arguments to them, they typically act defensively and incredulously.

I recall when, as a Baptist, I first learned that the Catholic Church opposed contraception. I thought it sheer lunacy. "What, is everyone supposed to have twenty children then?" My Baptist roommates felt the same way. I latched upon this Catholic doctrine and began to investigate it, because I was certain I could use it to discredit or even outright disprove that Catholicism was true.

I found some articles explaining the Catholic teachings, and though I wasn't convinced, I was impressed that Catholics had sensible-sounding arguments. I read more and became intrigued by the cohesiveness and beauty of the Church's teachings on marriage and sexuality in general. I then understood that the Church's opposition to contraception wasn't just a one-off rejection of modern technological "advances," but rather a reasoned stance within a much greater context of the dignity of the human person.

Other Protestants have actually been led into the Church by following this road. For one reason or another, they became uneasy with contraception. Then they started studying it and eventually discovered the Catholic Church's wisdom on this matter, opening the doors to Rome for them. So although I don't recommend contraception as the main topic of discussion to focus on with Protestant friends, it is one that can lead to fruitful discussion.

It is well-known that all Protestant denominations rejected contraception until the first half of the twentieth century.[35] Luther and many of the other key Reformers spoke forcefully against Christians imitating the sin of Onan (Gen. 38:8-10), and Bible Christians took seriously God's command to be fruitful (Gen. 1:28). But then, one-by-one, they toppled like dominoes, choosing to follow the spirit of the age rather than the Bible and their own religious traditions. I always point this fact out to Protestants, and for some it makes a big impact. Encourage them to find out when their own denomination reversed its teaching on contraception, and why.

Pope Paul VI predicted in *Humanae Vitae* the catastrophic

---

35. At the 1930 Lambeth Conference, the Church of England became the first Protestant denomination to say that contraception could be morally justified in some circumstances. How much things have changed since then!

repercussions, especially for women, that this sexual revolution would bring. And he has now been proven to be prophetic as Western society plunges into an ever deepening abyss of sexual confusion and moral degradation.

YOUR PRAYER TOGETHER
Litany of Humility.

READING RECOMMENDATIONS
• *The Bible and Birth Control,* by Charles D. Provan
• *Humanae Vitae,* by Pope Paul VI

18

WHEN THEIR ISSUE ISN'T YOUR ISSUE

Sometimes your Protestant friend will be bothered by an issue that seems unimportant to you. You listen to his concerns and dismiss them with what to you is a slam-dunk answer, but he is unconvinced and keeps bringing up the subject. These situations require you to dig deeper, both into the issue and into your store of patience. Let's look at three examples I have encountered, and how I dealt with them.

DISCIPLINE, OR THE LACK THEREOF

A cradle-Catholic-turned-Protestant friend named Jen messaged me with difficulties she had with the Catholic Church. In particular, she was appalled at the lack of moral discipline exercised by Catholic priests and bishops. She wrote:

> How does the Catholic Church ignore the New Testament's insistence on keeping the local assembly pure from the defilement of sin? For example, Paul's excommunication of the sinning man in 1 Corinthians [1 Cor. 5:1-13]. He does not just isolate this particular situation as unique, but further explains the general principle of dealing with sinful members of the Church. Those who call themselves brothers and yet are fornicators, sexually immoral, covetous, and thieves are to be removed from the fellowship of

the Church, delivered over to Satan, and excommunicated from the body of Christ.

I have seen Protestant churches do this, and it actually brings sinning people from a state of sin to repentance. A powerful conversion. And yet, as I told you I grew up Catholic, I don't believe I ever saw this nor do I think most Catholics today would even be aware that such a thing is required in the body of Christ.

Although I could see what Jen was saying, this issue had never been an important one for me. The only thing that mattered to me when I was investigating Catholicism was doctrine. How the Church exercises disciplinary authority over its members is a valuable topic to discuss, I thought, and certainly one where legitimate criticism can be made against many Catholic bishops and priests, but it is not one that I considered to be a foundational issue.

For instance, perhaps a priest should call out a local politician who publicly professes beliefs in direct contradiction to Catholic doctrine (for example, in favor of legal abortion), but if he failed to do so that didn't mean that the teachings of the Catholic Church were false. It just meant a priest failed to do his duty. (Or perhaps the priest called out the politician privately, or in some other way we just weren't aware of.)

I responded to Jen that, historically, the Church has used disciplines like excommunication more liberally than has been done in the past decades. And I agree with her that discipline should have the medicinal effect of bringing the sinner to repentance and return to full communion with Christ and his Church. But I emphasized that this was not a doctrinal issue.

I then brought the question back around to authority, the central issue. I wrote to her:

Realize too that, while some Protestant pastors or board of elders may "excommunicate" a person who goes to their church, where does their authority come from? How is it, exactly, that they can excommunicate someone? In the case of Congregationalists like Baptists, that person just leaves First Baptist and goes to Second Baptist and bam! he's back in communion with "the Church." So the question is: what constitutes the Church and how do I know if I am in full communion with it?

The Catholic Church answers this question cogently by pointing out that communion with the bishop of Rome (and the bishops in communion with him) is the authoritative standard for communion with the Church. In other words, Christ appointed rightful authorities on earth to lead his Church, and it is these men, and only these men, who have the authority to excommunicate someone. The Protestant model says that anyone who interprets the scriptures accurately has authority, but each person decides whether another interprets them accurately, so there is really no authority beyond the individual.

In situations like this one it is important to turn the spotlight back on Protestantism's lack of legitimate authority. Doing so shows that, even if Catholics aren't exercising discipline enough, at least they have the ability to properly exercise such biblical discipline. Protestant leaders may act as if they have such authority, but in fact they don't have it, and the ridiculousness of them pretending that they do is demonstrated in the fact that an "excommunicated" Protestant can just leave that church and be welcomed at the one down the street.

As always, be willing to concede valid points your friend makes. In this situation, I agree with Jen that Catholic bishops and priests should be exercising their rightful authority to discipline members of their flock, even to the point of excommunication. The failure of many bishops to discipline Catholics who flout the Church's teachings and promote grave evils is scandalous. That said, I am not a priest or bishop, do not know the situations in their full context, and believe that laity should be extremely careful in publicly criticizing clergy for using the discipline rod more liberally.

LIFELESS CATHOLICS AND VIBRANT PROTESTANTS

"Catholics seem dead to me," my Baptist friend Stephen said to me. "I go into my church, and I see life, vibrancy. But when I think about all the Catholics I know, you are one of the only ones who even acts like he believes in Jesus."

Stephen's perception is, sadly, all too common and understandable. If the Catholic Church is true, so the argument goes, why do many Catholics not seem to be living in a relationship with Christ? Why do so few know their faith, or read the Bible? Why do so few demonstrate a change in their lives?

Stephen described the situation this way:

> To me it seems that even if the people at a small Baptist church do not believe in many of the things taught in the early Church but are nonetheless living and keeping Christ's commands, they will enter the kingdom of God before many Catholics, even though the Catholics received all the sacraments.

His theory that vibrant Protestants enter the kingdom ahead of (or instead of) listless Catholics could be true. Jesus said he would spew out from his mouth lukewarm souls (Rev. 3:16). The sacraments are not magic. As one Catholic evangelist put it, Catholics have a billion dollars in the bank and most use a single dollar of it, while Baptists have just a hundred dollars in the bank, but most of them use all of it.

As with Church discipline, the issue of lifeless Catholics was not a big impediment to my conversion. In my mind, people were fallen sinners, and so even the true Church would have plenty of folks just going through the motions. But it was a monumental obstacle to my friend Stephen, and that is what matters. I did my best to help him realize that Protestant churches, too, have nominal members and "pew-warmers," and that this doesn't entail that Protestant teachings themselves are wrong. He agreed, but for him it was scandalous that Catholics in general lived lives that looked like non-Christians.

I also shared with him some of the reasons for the widespread loss of faith: the sexual revolution, the upheaval after the Second Vatican Council, the rise of secularism in the West, the increasingly hostile post-modern society we live in, and so on. These problems, I pointed out, have had a disastrous effect on *all* Christian churches and communities, including Protestant ones. He countered that, if Catholicism was the true Church, shouldn't it buck the prevailing trends more markedly than any other Christian group? It should, I agreed, and regarding doctrine and morals it has done so, but even the true Church is made up of human members, with all their faults.

Such issues are stumbling blocks for certain Protestants, particularly those who place a lot of stock in knowing a tree by its fruits. The best thing you can do is remind them that sin and human failings will always be with us, and then introduce them to Catholics who *are* living their faith. You can also share with them stories of faithful and intelligent Protestants becoming Catholic. I ended this talk with Stephen by smiling and saying, "You're right: there are lots of nominal and dead-looking Catholics. All the more reason we need you to become Catholic and help us evangelize those guys!"

TRANQUIL SEAS?

A third curveball you may get from your friend is not for him to fixate on something you find unimportant, but to be unconcerned about something you *do* find important. For example, some Protestants resist the Catholic Church because they think it ultimately doesn't matter what church you belong to. To them, "it's all good." Catholics are Christians; Protestants are Christians. Sure, we disagree on things, but none of those things are that important. We are already unified to a sufficient degree because we all believe in Jesus, and nothing more needs to be done.

My friend Kevin wrote to me expressing just this sentiment:

> Are there circles of heaven? Tiered planes for the different types of Christians? Is there more joy awaiting Catholics than non-Catholics? If so I could see some urgency in evangelizing non-Catholic Christians. But even if that was the case, it's heaven: you're not going to be aware of anything lacking; you won't be jealous of those that have more joy than you.

Even though the Catholic-Protestant differences looked serious to me, to him there was nothing to discuss between us.

You can *try* to make such people care, but the very nature of their indifferentism often makes them immune to theoretical argument. Often the best you can do is show them in word and deed how life-altering the consequences are of being Catholic versus Protestant. You may or may not succeed, but at least you can try.

Note that this road can go both ways. Sometimes you run into fellow Catholics who question why you are even worrying about bringing Protestants into full communion with the Catholic Church. "You should focus on atheists or non-Christians. Protestants already have the Holy Spirit and believe in the Trinity. Vatican II even said they'd be fine. You're wasting your time 'evangelizing' them," one friend enjoined me. One illustration must suffice of how life-changing it can be to share your Catholic faith with indifferent Protestants.

My friend Brandon had been going with his wife to a nondescript Protestant church for several years. He and I had never spoken about religion because I never got the sense from him that it was important to him. However, one day a political discussion sprang up between us, and it led to a conversation about morality, in particular about the sanctity of human life.

Brandon and his wife had one daughter at the time. She wasn't baptized, and he wasn't sure if she should be. The church they were at placed little to no emphasis on baptism, so they just kept going along with the current, slowly floating, metaphorically speaking, with the lazy river of choose-your-own-adventure Protestantism.

The conversation that we had, though, sparked another conversation. I was doing my utmost to persuade him to care about the humanity of unborn children. He was amenable to the idea in general, and over time he came to be firmly pro-life. At that point, he began to wonder about his Protestant church, as I continued to gently prod him on what he believed and why.

By God's grace, his conscience was pricked, and he started to study what his denomination taught and why. He learned its origins—an Englishman in the 1800s dissatisfied with the existing Protestant buffet—and made the decision to leave their church. Though we had discussed Catholicism for six months, he wasn't ready to become Catholic. Instead, he and his wife joined an Episcopal church.

Brandon and I kept talking, and after three years of prayer and discussion, he and his wife made the decision to become Catholic. They entered full communion, along with their daughter, who was baptized and received first Communion.

Subsequently, they had two more children and have been involved in multiple apostolates at their church, from music to men's retreats to RCIA. Their gentle spirits have blossomed in the Church and been a blessing to many within it.

Even indifferent Protestants can be moved by grace. See if God opens up a door with friends of yours like Brandon, and simply take one step at a time toward helping them discover the truth.

YOUR PRAYER TOGETHER
The *Anima Christi*.

RECOMMENDED READING
1 Corinthians chapter 5

19

STRANGE CREATURES OF THE DEEP

IN THE COURSE of your own life's voyage, you will doubtless find yourself running into some Protestants with very odd beliefs, and not be prepared to dialogue with them in ways you've encountered or practiced before. In this chapter we're going to look at two people that I have run into who shared a peculiarly similar oddness of biblical interpretation.

BIBLE PREACHER MAN

I met Jason, a new coworker, and was delighted to find out he was a Christian. Several of us went out to lunch and one of my agnostic friends, who through my discussions with him had come to understand the differences between Protestants and Catholics, asked Jason what he believed. It was a bit of a baiting by my agnostic friend, hoping that I would then sink the hook in him and we'd have an exciting debate.

"Oh, I believe in the Bible. Straight Bible from Jesus," Jason said.

"But why not be Catholic?" my friend asked him.

"Catholics, well, you have to realize that they're off on their beliefs. Some of them are Christians, but their teachings are not biblical."

Amid such mixed company, including several atheists, I chose not to take up the discussion at that time. But over the next few months I broached the subject of faith with Jason. He was a sincere guy with a great sense of humor.

One morning I left of a copy of my book, *The Protestant's Dilemma*, on his desk. He arrived to work and started looking at it, so I swung by and told him it was a gift to him. He said that he would read it. And I left it at that.

A few weeks later, Jason told me that he and his wife had been told about some great videos from a Bible preacher and that he was learning tons from it. "This guy is great," Jason said, "because every single thing he teaches comes *straight* from the Bible."

I nodded appreciatively and asked Jason the guy's name. He told me, and I looked him up. Now, remember that there is no Protestant who preaches straight truth from the Bible. They all claim to; they all think they do; but none of them actually do it. Because in truth, the Bible isn't perspicacious in all places, so anyone who teaches from it, sooner or later, is going to be teaching his own interpretations. It's inevitable. Either you teach from the Church's apostolic Tradition, or you teach according to your own human tradition. (And Protestants agree that Jesus condemned human traditions.)

The preacher that Jason and his wife were listening to was a Mid-Acts Hyper-Dispensationalist Protestant. To go into what that exactly means would take several chapters. The short version is that such Protestants interpret the Bible to mean that the Church we know of today did not start until somewhere in the middle of the book of Acts, when St. Paul began his ministry. They posit that there was a Hebrew or Jewish Church that existed up until the middle of Acts, but that this gave way (i.e., a new dispensation) to the real Church, which taught that people are saved by grace through faith alone. Interestingly, in this theory St. Paul in many ways takes precedence over Jesus in terms of theology and teaching.

Now, this is a niche belief even within Protestantism. You may go your entire life without running into one of these folks. I only knew about it because I had run into another variety of this type of Protestant some years prior, in a story we'll examine in the second part of this chapter.

The material point to take away, however, is that my friend and his wife were taking as gospel truth the opinions of a man who is in a subset of a niche of a corner of Protestantism. I sent my friend Jason a message gently explaining that this preacher's beliefs were only a century or so old, novelties even among Protestantism's denominations. I warned him to be on guard about what he accepted from this man. And I helped him see that, while the man claimed to teach "Bible truth," really he taught his own opinions about what the Bible said.

Jason listened to what I told him but was skeptical of it. Already in his short Christian life he had become biased against something a Catholic would tell him while blindly accepting fringe Protestant opinions. Still, the seed was planted. He would at least begin to question whether what such preachers so confidently proclaimed to be biblical was in fact the true interpretation of the Bible.

Protestantism being what it is, not infrequently you will encounter Protestants who buy into a tradition that seems far less plausible than Catholicism, yet they swallow it hook, line, and sinker. This goes for many Protestant denominations, from the dispensationalists in this chapter to Pastor Jimmy-Bob preaching out of his house church, but it also includes quasi-Christian sects such as the Jehovah's Witnesses, Mormons, and Seventh-Day Adventists.

When you meet such people, remember the fundamental principles of arguing for Catholicism: the Church was founded by Christ and he protects it from error. All these sects have to deny that claim and supply an apostasy or heresy story that results in their sect restoring "true Christianity" centuries upon centuries later. The Catholic claim is biblically supportable and more plausible.

MY PATIENCE RAN OUT BEFORE THE BOOK OF ACTS DID

A Catholic friend of mine requested that I dialogue with a Protestant friend of hers. Kirk was the Protestant guy's name, and I and another Catholic evangelist began a discussion over email with him. Kirk was friendly in his messages, but from the start communicated to us that he was an "Acts 28 Hyper-Dispensationalist."

I learned that this type of dispensationalist is considered "Late-Acts" to differentiate them from the "Mid-Acts" variety that we met previously in this chapter. They believe that the Church did not start until the very *end* of Acts, with St. Paul's indication that Israel rejected the kingdom of God and that salvation was going out to the Gentiles:

> When they had appointed a day for him, they came to him at his lodging in great numbers. And he expounded the matter to them from morning till evening, testifying to the kingdom of God and trying to convince them about Jesus both from the law of Moses and from the prophets. And some were convinced by what he said, while others disbelieved. So, as they disagreed among themselves, they departed, after Paul had made one statement: "The Holy Spirit was right in saying to your fathers through Isaiah the prophet:
>
> 'Go to this people, and say, You shall indeed hear but never understand, and you shall indeed see but never perceive. For this people's heart has grown dull, and their ears are heavy of hearing, and their eyes they have closed; lest they should perceive with their eyes, and hear with their

ears, and understand with their heart, and turn for me to heal them.' Let it be known to you then that this salvation of God has been sent to the Gentiles; they will listen" (Acts 28:23–28).

Kirk explained that, due to his dispensationalist beliefs, he also rejected water baptism. Late-Acts Hyper-Dispensationalists also look at the four Gospels and Jesus' words as applying to Israel and not to them and the Church, since they allege that those writings applied only to the older dispensation that has now been superseded. These Protestants believe many things, then, that are quite strange to Catholics (and even to other Protestants), and their beliefs find no basis in the early Church itself or in the writings of the Fathers.

Kirk was ready to duke it out and trade Bible verse punches, and mentioned that he had debated a Catholic previously on the question of God's divine foreknowledge. I wasn't game for that, for I knew it wouldn't go anywhere. So I tried using plausibility arguments instead, pointing out that his beliefs were so novel and peculiar that it would mean everyone in Christianity—including the Protestants!—had gotten fundamental doctrines wrong for 1,900 years. Such a position is substantially similar to Mormonism's idea of a Great Apostasy: that the Church went apostate for 1,800 years before "true Christianity" was rediscovered.

He took umbrage at my line of argument and told me that he felt I was being dismissive of him, trying to bypass the Bible entirely. I responded that my experience indicated trading verses in such a situation was not often profitable. He was frustrated with my statements and attitude in general. For my part, I had a hard time taking his beliefs seriously.

I bowed out of the discussion and messaged the other Catholic on the email thread, wishing him God's blessing as he continued the discussion. I admitted that I didn't have the grace to argue with Kirk. Reflecting on it later, I realized that I should have excused myself from the conversation even earlier, once I understood how fringe his ideas were.

We are not called to get into a deep discussion with every Protestant who crosses our path. In this case, a very capable fellow Catholic was willing to engage him already. I didn't have the patience to spend hours in discussion with such a person where the battleground was unlikely to help us make progress toward unity in the truth. Sometimes it is better to just leave a conversation with prayers for the person on the other side.

RECOMMENDED READING
The Apostasy That Wasn't, by Rod Bennett

CONCLUSION

Coming in to Port

MOST TIMES WE plant seeds. Oftentimes we water. But occasionally our Lord gives us the grace of getting to bring in
the harvest.

You may find yourself in the happy position of seeing your
Protestant friend soften toward the Catholic Church, become
convinced of its truth, and decide to enter full communion.
Rejoice! This is a great gift, for you and for him, and one that
we give God the glory and thanks for.

Bringing the ship into harbor can be tricky business,
though. And even once in the harbor, the waves can hit the
dock while they're disembarking on terra firma. Your job
doesn't end when your friend decides to be Catholic, or even
after he has entered the Church. He will need you during
these last three stages of the journey just as much as the first.

PHASE I: APPROACHING SHORE

Your friend is getting close. You've seen signs that he is
warming up to the Church. He understands the arguments,
has been praying, and is beginning to see that the Catholic
Church might just be what it claims to be.

This is an exciting but delicate time. Be careful not to
smother your friend; give him the space he needs. Be ready to
answer any questions and offer friendship and spiritual support, but watch to see if he draws back some, and be prepared
to leave space for the Holy Spirit to close the deal.

Here is where the mystery of the human heart and the
workings of the Spirit most powerfully come together. Satan

does not want him to become Catholic, does not want him to receive the Eucharist and be confirmed, does not want him to receive Confession and enter fully into the life of faith in the Church. But God does. And God is stronger.

With one friend who reached this point I had to back way off, because in addition to becoming Catholic, he was having to admit that I was "right" and he was wrong. For some, swallowing their pride is not difficult, but for others it can be one of the last obstacles. Your celebration is not in being right, but in being used as an instrument of our Lord to bring a soul into his Church.

PHASE 2: COMING INTO PORT

Now, he has made his decision and told you he wants to be Catholic. What do you do next? Typically, he speaks to the pastor of the local parish and inquires into its RCIA program.

Sometimes the timing works out: it's fall, RCIA is about to begin, and he is able to start immediately and be received into the Church at Easter Vigil the following year. Other times it doesn't quite fall so perfectly and a period of waiting might have to begin. Encourage your friend to talk with a deacon or priest at the parish to find out if there are any options for receiving instruction if the waiting period before the next RCIA class is going to be lengthy. (One friend of mine could not make it to RCIA regularly due to his family and work duties. He informed the priest of his situation, and he was able to receive private instruction with the priest and members of the RCIA team at times that worked with his particular schedule.)

Perhaps he has asked you to be his sponsor. Now you can go to RCIA together, allowing you to supplement (and perhaps at times, unfortunately, correct) the instruction he receives there, and continue to be a good Catholic friend.

During this time he is also having to share the news of his upcoming conversion with his friends and family. This can be the most difficult of all steps for a convert. He may have Protestant loved ones—including members of his church—who are shocked and disturbed that he is becoming Catholic. They may send him books, videos, show up at his house, and even call him before the board of elders at his church. The pastor may visit him; his friends will email him with long messages explaining all the evils of Catholicism in hopes of convincing him to change his mind.

He may even waver at this onslaught. Many Protestants have had fear of Catholicism indoctrinated into them from early childhood. He'll be accused of worshiping Mary, praying to dead people, taking glory from God, earning his salvation by works, and a hundred other errors and misconceptions that his Protestant friends still have, and that he himself may have had up until recently.

If this situation happens with your friend, encourage him to share with you any fears he has. He may want to forward you particular emails that he has received for help in answering them. Just because he is becoming Catholic doesn't mean he knows he has heard every argument against Catholicism, let alone knows the rejoinder to it. Go fishing together on the shores of the Tiber—Castel Sant'Angelo at your back—and search and find the answers to challenges that he may be presented with.

Sadly, many converts from Protestantism see many of their friends and family cut off those relationships. I lost many friends, men I considered as close as brothers, and it cut me to the quick. He may lose friends too. Encourage him not to burn bridges, and to try to see ahead to a time when tempers settle and people see that he is still the good man that they knew, only now Catholic.

PHASE 3: THE TIBER IS CROSSED

Your friend has become Catholic. He has entered full communion. It is the ending of his journey across the Tiber, but it
is the beginning of a much greater journey, one that will last
him his whole life.

I wish you could tell him that it's all downhill from here,
that it will be easy and pleasant. But we know that that is not
the case. You still have a role to play, both as a friend but also
as a guide to a neophyte in the wide land that is Catholicism.

Encourage him to dive deep: adoration, learning about the
saints, daily Mass, devotions. He may even need to leave the
arguments and apologetics aside for a while. I know I did.
I wanted to explore, to immerse myself in the Faith, not to
argue fine points.

Suggest that he consider getting to know fellow Catholics by getting involved: Knights of Columbus, men's groups,
Society of St. Vincent de Paul, or just helping with the parish
seasonal festivals. The goal is to help him get connected to the
Catholic community and for him to have the opportunity to
serve the Church and the world as a Catholic.

Be prepared that he may face disappointment, or even
disillusionment. We know that the Catholic Church here on
earth is made up of people, and people can be selfish, rude,
and inconsiderate. That can be jarring. Also, some liturgies are
celebrated with appropriate reverence and beauty; others are
done in a sloppy and slipshod way.

He may encounter Catholics who don't believe in all that
the Church teaches. I recall becoming Catholic and having a
nun—one of the first I had ever met—tell me that women
should be priests. I was shocked, and gently reminded her that
the Catholic Church teaches that only men can be priests.
She gave me a knowing look, amused by my naiveté, and
suggested to me that such teachings could be changed. He

should be prepared to meet such Catholics and not have his faith shaken when he does.

Depending upon his state of life, you could encourage him to discern his vocation. If he is single, suddenly a new option has opened up: priesthood or consecrated religious life. This is a great gift, one that did not exist for him as a Protestant. It may or may not be the right time for him to think about such things—you as a friend will know whether to broach the topic or not—but you should keep it in mind as something to introduce him to.

Finally, keep being a good friend to him. The bond you have forged as a Catholic who led him into full communion is unique, and the effects eternal. While you may not remain close friends your entire life, you will always have this special connection.

YOUR PRAYER TOGETHER
The Angelus or *Regina Coeli*.

RECOMMENDED READING:
Filling Our Father's House, by Shaun McAfee

POSTSCRIPT

The River Winds On

YOU HAVE BEEN helping your friend navigate the Tiber for a long time—weeks, months, perhaps years of conversations. You have argued with him, exchanged countless Bible verses and book recommendations, prayed with him and for him.

And your friend is probably still Protestant. Does that mean you have failed? Not necessarily.

For most, the way of conversion is long, stretching and winding like the Tiber River itself. You may not see them reach the end of it and become Catholic. But that's not your worry: you have shared the Catholic faith with them, prayed for them, and been a good friend to them. That's the most that we can do.

It always has been and always is God's grace that moves hearts. A mystery exists between your friend's heart and God's invitation, and only he knows how it will end.

I worked with a guy for five years before we started hanging out together as friends. I got to know him and discovered he was reared in the churches of Christ but then became an unprogrammed Quaker. We began talking about the Christian faith and Catholicism, and the discussion went on for months, and then years. He became an Episcopalian at one point, which was a big move for him, since the services are liturgical. Eventually I moved to a different town, and we couldn't get together regularly. But a year after that he and his wife became Catholic. Our friendship had been going on for ten years, and our discussions for five. Numerous were the times I wrote him off; he seemed so far away, and yet our Lord hadn't written him off. God was always working, invisibly, behind the scenes, in my friend's heart, and I witnessed the fruits of his work firsthand as my friend's Confirmation sponsor.

Another friend of mine was an agnostic or perhaps a weak deist when we met. After five years he became a Christian, going to an Emergent Protestant church. He and I had discussions every week for the next four years. He couldn't see how Catholicism could be true. He always had objections, but he was an avid reader. He read theological blogs and books from across the Christian spectrum. Eventually he learned my arguments so well that when we had lunch with another Protestant friend he would take my side of the argument and play "Catholic's advocate," almost always providing cogent answers to our mutual friend!

I took the long-term approach with him. We were friends regardless; we enjoyed each other's company, and we had many mutual interests. One day, out of the blue, he told me

---

INVITE!

Be creative in how you engage with your Protestant friends. The Catholic faith is rich, deep, and beautiful. Here are three tips for you to consider:

1. Pray for them and ask them to pray with you. It could be the Hail Mary, Our Father, Divine Mercy Chaplet, the Rosary, or just spontaneous prayers (which may be more comfortable for them)

2. After discernment, consider asking them if they want to come to Mass with you. Help them feel comfortable ahead of time by explaining different parts of the Mass, giving them a Magnificat or other aide that helps them understand what to do when.

3. Invite them to vespers, compline, a prayer service, or anything else going on that you think would help them

4. Invite them to eucharistic adoration. I have known people who came before Jesus present in the Blessed Sacrament and "knew" that Jesus was there. Let God do the converting for you!

he thought Catholicism was true. He started going to RCIA and finding out what he needed to do to become Catholic. He began a running joke whenever we got together: he'd punch me in the shoulder and say, "Rose, why didn't you ever tell me that Catholicism was true?" People have to work through the questions and issues in their own way and time.

The path we traveled is just one of many. There is no one right way here, no dogmatic decree about how to have dialogue with your non-Catholic friends. The Church wisely realizes that the complexities of people and relationships mean that it is best to let the Holy Spirit move in the way he wants in these discussions. It is up to us as Catholics to be attentive to the Spirit and follow where and how he leads in our friendships.

I have seen the lights go on in my Protestant friends' eyes when they saw something about Catholicism that they didn't notice before. I've also seen the thoughtful, unsettled look trouble them when I presented an argument on the canon or the sacraments that they don't have an answer to. The path we traveled here, wending about though it did, was all meant to provoke that look—to place before them Catholic truth in a way that leaves them open to the Holy Spirit's promptings within. Don't get discouraged. When you do, it likely means you were relying on yourself more than on God, expecting your brilliant arguments to be so compelling that your friend would convert instantly. I've done that more times than I care to remember. Changing our theological paradigm, or even contemplating doing so, is a difficult action for anyone to take. It should not be done willy-nilly and usually isn't. So set your expectations for a long haul.

Don't be triumphalistic (as, sadly, I sometimes have been). The Catholic Church may indeed be the fullness of the truth, but that doesn't mean that we its members are perfect. Far too often we sin and fall short of the holy life Christ calls us to. Stay close to the Church, receive the sacraments, seek to remain in a state of grace, that you might not be disqualified after working so hard to bring your friends into full communion. Some friends of mine, even after they decided to become Catholic, were loath to tell me, since I could then smirk about how "I was right all along." What a terrible thing! Yet it happened. Fortunately their jubilation at becoming Catholic overcame their reluctance to tell me. I'm learning slowly to practice what I preach.

Be a great friend. Little good it does to have the right argument if you fail in friendship. Does he need help moving? Get up early on Saturday and help him. Are you asking him about how his life is going, his struggles, and his hopes? Do so. Don't just blather on about your own stuff, though in any friendship there will be a back-and-forth exchange of talking and listening. Apologize when you overstep your bounds or say something that comes off hurtfully. A little humility goes a long way.

Finally, place your trust in the Lord, who made heaven and earth. He loves your friend more than you do and desires that he be fully united to his Church. He's the most powerful ally you can have, and you do have him. God works in ways we don't see and never ceases to surprise us. So believe with all your might and love with all your heart. God will supply every grace needed, and bring about that perfect unity that Jesus prayed for in the seventeenth chapter of St. John's Gospel: "that they may all be one." May it be done unto us, according to his word.

ABOUT THE AUTHOR

DEVIN ROSE converted from atheism to Evangelical Protestantism in college. Some years later he became Catholic and since then has had a mission to help Catholics lead their Protestant friends into full communion with the Church. He is a computer programmer and lives with his wife and children in central Texas. His book *The Protestant's Dilemma* is published by Catholic Answers Press.